"Sometimes in our troubles, we call out, thinking no one hears. But God always hears!"

"After years of pastoring Derek Quan knows the deep questions people are asking. This is why Pastor Quan can bring to us biblical wisdom that will feed the soul and calm the heart. I highly recommend your reading reflectively this gift to the church."
Dr. DARRYL DELHOUSSAYE, President, Phoenix Seminary

"Dr. Quan's book, *The Faithful and the Flawed*, is an excellent source of encouragement for the Christ-follower who seeks to learn life-lessons from some of the major personalities recorded in Scripture. Utilizing sound Biblical exegesis and practical application, the reader is swept into the Biblical narrative in a way that informs and inspires! A great devotional book that can also be used in a small group Bible Study!"
Dr. LARRY VOLD, Senior Pastor, Neighborhood Church, Castro Valley, CA.

"In *The Faithful and the Flawed*, Derek examines the lives of Biblical characters and produces insightful life applications, drawing from his years of pastoral experience and his skill in studying Scripture. The reader will tremendously enjoy learning and reflecting on this devotional."
Rev. KUANG-FU YANG, Senior Pastor, Greater Phoenix Chinese Christian Church

"*The Faithful and the Flawed* is filled with lots of wise insights drawn from the Word of God. You'll find this an enjoyable and challenging book to read because Derek draws us into the Bible and makes clear its relevance to our lives. I highly recommend the book."
Dr. NORM WAKEFIELD, Professor Emeritus, Phoenix Seminary

The Faithful and The Flawed

Learning Life Lessons From Those Who Came Before Us

Derek Quan

Intermedia Publishing Group

The Faithful and the Flawed
Learning Life Lessons From Those Who Came Before Us

Copyright ©2011
By Derek Quan

Published by:
Intermedia Publishing Group
PO Box 2825
Peoria, AZ 85380
www.intermediapub.com

Scripture quotations marked NLT are taken from the *Holy Bible*, New Living Translation, copyright © 1996, 2004. Used by permission of Tyndale House Publishers, Inc., Wheaton, Ill 60189. All rights reserved.

Scripture quotations marked TLB or The Living Bible are taken from The Living Bible / Kenneth N. Taylor. electronic ed. Wheaton Ill 60189: Tyndale House, 1997, c1971 by Tyndale House Publishers, Inc. Used by permission. All rights reserved.

Scripture taken from the Message, Copyright © 1993, 1994, 1996, 2000, 2001, 2002. Used by permission of NavPress Publishing Group

ISBN 978-1-935529-20-0

Printed in the United States of America

All rights reserved.

No part of this publication may be reproduced, stored in a retrieval system or transmitted in any form or by any means — electronic, mechanical, digital photocopy, recording, or any other without the prior written permission of the author.

About the Author

Derek Quan, a native of Northern California, moved to Chandler, AZ, to pastor at Greater Phoenix Chinese Christian Church in 1993. He has a Bachelor's degree in Fine Arts from Cal-State University, Hayward (Now East Bay), and a Master's in Business Administration from Santa Clara University. He worked for Mervyn's, a soft goods retailer, for eleven years before beginning full-time pastoral ministry. He received his Master of Divinity degree from Western Seminary and his Doctor of Ministry degree from Phoenix Seminary, where he served on the board from 2001 to 2005. He is married to Kathy and they have two daughters, Bethany and Rebekah.

Contents

Acknowledgements xi
Foreword xiii
Abraham 1
Sarah 21
Elizabeth 41
Cain 61
David 81
Jephthah 105
Samson 125
Barnabas 145
Nehemiah 165
Daniel 187
Conclusion 209

"Therefore, since we are surrounded by such a great cloud of witnesses, let us throw off everything that hinders and the sin that so easily entangles, and let us run with perseverance the race marked out for us."[3]

---

[3] Hebrews 12:2 NIV

Acknowledgements

I count it a privilege to have pastored in the same church since 1993. I love most of the tasks and responsibilities that come with the call, but one that I'm not too fond of is coming up with annual goals and objectives.

One of them that has been on my plate for the last five years is writing a book. I had the best of intentions, but sermon preparation, Bible studies, board meetings, and fellowship gatherings, as priorities, squeezed out the desire to write a book...my first book.

Well, with a little help from my family and friends, I am glad to announce that this book has finally come to fruition.

First of all, I want to thank my church family at Greater Phoenix Chinese Christian Church, Chandler, AZ, for being such a great and loving congregation. I have never lacked for friends or fellow coworkers. They have encouraged and challenged me to grow not only in ability, but in character as well.

Second, I want to thank my family. My wife, Kathy, whom all would acknowledge is the better half of this marriage, is a gift from heaven. It sounds corny, but she really does complete me. Thanks for your patience, honey. God's not done with me yet. Then there are my two "Daddy's girls," Bethany and Rebekah. They are the joy and pride of my life. I pray that they will someday do something great for our God and for his Kingdom.

Third, I want to thank those at Intermedia Publishing Group, especially Jon McHatton. God providentially brought us together in a seminary parking lot, and through his encouragement and follow through, I was able to focus on completing this book. I also want to thank my editor, Karen Hsu, for doing an incredible job of cleaning up my manuscript.

Finally, I want to thank the Lord Jesus Christ for coming into my life so many years ago. He saved me when I needed a Savior. He gave me purpose when I had no clue what life was about. He called me in spite of my many flaws. Thank you, Lord Jesus!

Foreword

Faith is a funny word. As Christ-followers, many of us use the term with unconscious regularity, but seldom question of what substance faith really is. Here's what the writer of the book of Hebrews says of faith:

> *"What is faith? It is the confident assurance that something we want is going to happen. It is the certainty that what we hope for is waiting for us, even though we cannot see it up ahead."*[1]
>
> *"The act of faith is what distinguished our ancestors, set them above the crowd."*[2]

Faith is an intangible, something not directly grasped or seen in and of itself, but is manifested through God's people in how they live. The Scriptures not only contain statements about faith, but it is also a written record of individuals who triumphed in staying true to God, as well as those who floundered and fell short of remaining true.

As a pastor who has had the privilege of preaching and shepherding since 1993, I've found that most of my sermons have influenced me much more than most of those in my

---

[1] Hebrews 11:1 TLB
[2] Hebrews 11:2 The Message

congregation. But regardless of the audience, the messages that have probably had the most impact in touching hearts are the ones that relate to the faith manifested and tested by men and women in the Scriptures.

This book presents ten of these individuals, outlining their myriad of challenges and triumphs that have drawn the empathy, as well as sympathy, of countless believers throughout the ages. We identify with these men and women who have struggled to maintain a godly faith. It is my desire that God would touch your heart and help you to realize you're not alone, that Christian followers before you have had the same fears, challenges and trials, and have conquered them through faith.

This book is meant to be read devotionally, and can be used either for your own edification or in a group setting. Before you begin to read a chapter, take time to pray and ask God's Spirit to reveal how you and/or your friends might apply the truths to your life. At the end of each chapter, there are Memory Verses, Application Questions, and Heartwork, suggestions on how you might put some of the principles learned into practice.

I thank the Lord for the privilege of communicating God's timeless truths through the experience of those men and women who came before us. May we learn from their lives and move forward in faith.

For His Kingdom,

Derek Quan
Pastor
Greater Phoenix Chinese Christian Church
Chandler, AZ

Abraham

Faith to Believe in the Impossible
Genesis 22

It's amazing the kind of information that is readily available from the internet. When my wife Kathy and I found out that she was pregnant, we came across a website that gave weekly updates telling us what was happening in the womb at that moment. On the fourteenth week, what is considered to be the end of the first trimester, the site explained that many expectant mothers wait until this time to share with their employers that they're pregnant. The rationale for waiting this long is not so much about giving out career-limiting information, but rather, that during the first trimester is when there is the greatest chance for miscarriage. The logic of not telling your boss, your parents, or anyone else for that matter, is that if you lose the baby through miscarriage, since they didn't know about the pregnancy in the first place, they won't be disappointed with your loss.

Kathy and I realized that there was a chance for miscarriage, especially since it was our first child; but as soon as we knew, we told our congregation (after our parents and siblings) that we were expecting a baby. The reason we shared our good news so early was because we believed that the fervent prayers of the saints were more important than the possible disappointment of a miscarriage.

All you have to do is glance at the front section of your daily newspaper or read the headlines off Yahoo news to realize how frightening it is to raise a child in today's world. As new parents-to-be, we hear about child abuse, kidnappings, pool drownings, poisoning, SIDS (Sudden Infant Death Syndrome), and the like, and it terrifies us.

So every night, we would place our hands on Kathy's abdomen and pray for our baby's health and future safety. In addition, we continued to pray in faith that God would bless this child, which Baby Q would grow up to be a godly person, walking with and serving the Lord. We realized at that time, and even today, that there are no guarantees. You can raise your child to the absolute best of your ability and bad things can still happen. And yet, ultimately, our faith is in a gracious God who had blessed our desire to have a child. We believed in faith that God brought about Kathy's pregnancy. The challenge after conception was would we have the same faith to believe that what God had begun, he would bring about to righteous completion?

Unswerving Faith

Faith is an interesting word. Church folk throw the word around without, many times, thinking about what they're talking about. We'll speak of the missionary who's been overseas for three decades, who has only had two converts, and speak of her as a woman of great faith. Or we'll note the father who has had difficulty finding a job, and he begins to doubt that God will provide. We call him a man of little faith. We hear of the five year old whose father has abandoned the family, and the tyke believes with all of her heart that Jesus will bring Daddy back. We call it child-like faith.

What Is Faith?

Great faith, little faith, child-like faith. Faith seems to come in all kinds of flavors. But really, what is faith? Probably the best working definition of faith is found in the Bible itself. The writer of Hebrews says, *"Now faith is being sure of what we hope for and certain of what we do not see."*[4]

You can't read it in English, but in the original Greek, the verb "is" speaks of a present and continual reality. Simply put, faith is not merely a virtue, but rather, it is a condition which is to be lived out continually. One writer says this of faith:

> "Faith signifies that there are realities for which we have no material evidence though they are not the less real for that. Faith enables us to know that they exist and, while we have no certainty apart from faith, faith does give us genuine certainty. Faith, then becomes the basis, the substructure of all that the Christian life means, all that the Christian hopes for. We can't see God, we can't touch him, we can't even hear an audible voice, but by faith we know he is with us, guiding us, working out his sovereign plan of which we are a part."[5]

---

[4] Hebrews 11:1 NIV
[5] Leon Morris, *Expositor's Bible Commentary*

The author of Hebrews begins in chapter 11 by defining what faith is, how it will manifest itself, and then spends the rest of the chapter giving examples of individuals who displayed this kind of unswerving faith. Abraham, the hero of this chapter, had faith. In verses 8 – 9, it says that, *"By faith Abraham, when called to go to a place he would later receive as his inheritance, obeyed and went, even though he did not know where he was going."*

Getting To Know Abraham

For those of us who grew up in children's Sunday School, we know all about Abraham, the father of the Israelites...that is we know about this godly man *after he left for Canaan*. But we don't discuss much what Abraham was like before he left his native land of Ur. The simple truth is that Abraham, before he met God, was nothing special. Like those in his surrounding community, he was just another Pagan. Certainly, he had an outstanding reputation among his peers because of his wealth and social standing. The above verse tells us that when God called Abraham to leave his community and go to Canaan, he would be blessed with even more land. Abraham was considered faithful because he believed that this God who spoke to him would fulfill his promise. So his faith was manifested and he moved his wife and servants to God's Promised Land.

You may be thinking, well, that's nice. It is an act of faith to up and leave and replant myself in a different land. And perhaps this faith could be characterized as somewhat extraordinary in that Abraham and his wife were senior citizens. How many of our parents or grandparents who live on social security or a meager retirement would pull up roots and move from their home town? Not many. So we would have to agree that Abraham demonstrated faith; perhaps we could even call it *strong* faith. But if we were honest, most of us wouldn't consider what he did to be a manifestation of *incredible* faith.

Uprooting yourself and moving on to greener pastures doesn't seem that extraordinary, especially since most Americans have done or are willing to do it. The 2000 census reaffirmed that many in our society are moving from the Midwest and Northeast to the West, Southwest, and South, from the Rust Belt to the Sun Belt. The factors for this mass migration include searching for a better job, living in a milder climate, or increasing the standard of living. But the bottom line is a move to another area to better your life is not that big of a deal. So if we were to judge Abraham's faith on this factor alone, it's probably not that significant.

> **We might have credible faith to believe in the *financially feasible*; but it takes incredible faith, supernatural faith, to believe in the *biologically impossible*.**

However, the writer of Hebrews goes on and explains that Abraham demonstrated an even greater faith. In verses 11 – 12, he continues that,

> *"By faith Abraham, even though he was past age – and Sarah herself was barren – was enabled to become a father because he considered him faithful who had made the promise. And so from this one man, and he as good as dead,*

came descendants as numerous as the stars in the sky and as countless as the sand on the seashore."

We might have credible faith to believe in the *financially feasible*; but it takes incredible faith, supernatural faith, to believe in the *biologically impossible*.

A Deeper Level of Faith

Sarah's womb was dead. Lifeless and without the means to nourish an unborn child; it was physically impossible for her to have children. On top of that, Mrs. Abraham was very old. She was still ten years younger than her husband, but at ninety, it was physiologically impossible for her to bear children.

You may be a person who watches a Christian television network on a regular basis, and you've witnessed those healing crusades. Honesty necessitates that I admit that I'm a little skeptical of these gatherings because, quite frankly, the ones that I see usually being "healed" are individuals with limps, or who purport to have arthritis, are mute, or have lived with back pain their whole lives. These people who give testimony are then touched by the faith healer's hand (many of these ministers give the glory to God), and suddenly, the lame walk, the mute shouts, the pain disappears, the cancer vanishes. And as brothers and sisters in Christ, we rejoice with these individuals.

But maybe I'm a person of little faith. These kinds of so-called healings are biologically possible. What I want to see is the physiologically impossible. I want someone to wheel up a pair of Siamese twins who are joined at the head and, at these faith healings, I want them to be miraculously split apart. Or I'd like to see a child born with cerebral palsy able to gain full functionality instantaneously. Most of all, I want to see someone who has been pronounced clinically dead, no breath, no brain wave, no pulse, to suddenly come back to life and shout, "Hallelujah!"

At this moment, you could counter that bringing life back to a corpse is a biological impossibility. And you'd be right. That's why it takes incredible faith to believe that it can be done. But the amazing aspect of Abraham's faith is that he believed God could heal Sarah's dead womb. And God fulfilled his promise by giving Abraham and Sarah the promised son, Isaac.

This son, Isaac, was the child born of the promise. I'm sure that as Abraham looked down at his baby boy, his heart welled up with joy. As he cradled the newborn in his arms, as little Ike's hand grabbed a hold of his father's gnarly pinky finger, I'm sure, the patriarch with joyful tears in his eyes was thanking the Lord out loud for this special blessing. This old man felt energized again. This child would be the fulfillment of the Lord's promise to make Abraham's descendents number like the sands on the seashore.

We have a God who fulfills his promises. And as a God of promise, the Lord is faithful to us – faithful to the point that he will even remove that which would prevent His will from being accomplished.

> **The Lord is faithful to the point that he will even remove that which would prevent His will from being accomplished.**

We witness this truth in Abraham's older son, Ishmael, who was born through his Egyptian maidservant Hagar.

Perhaps it was out of jealousy, the text doesn't say, but Genesis 21 records that Ishmael mocked his little stepbrother. Sarah took notice of this transgression and, ever the protective mother, commanded Abraham to send Hagar and her beastly little child away. It seems like such an extreme action to take, especially when we take into account that it was actually Sarah who insisted that Abraham sleep with her maidservant Hagar in the first place. (By the way, we'll be looking at Sarah and Hagar more in the next chapter). But God understands our hearts and he's willing to work around our pettiness, jealousy and unrighteous ways, and accomplish His will. Hindsight always being 20/20, it was most likely a good thing to send Hagar and Ishmael away because Isaac needed all the protection he could get.

The days passed into weeks, the weeks into months, and the months into years. Isaac was eventually weaned, began to learn how to take care of himself, found his place in the community, and before you knew it, he became a strapping teenager. I'm sure there wasn't a day that didn't go by where Abraham and Sarah thanked the Lord for giving them this wonderful son. Through the Lord's enabling, Isaac would someday become a great man.

Abraham's faithfulness was paying off. He trusted the Lord from the very beginning, and God rewarded the patriarch's faithfulness with a settlement in the most fertile of land. Abraham trusted God with his wife's dead womb, and God further blessed him with this handsome, strong son. Abraham's faith was met every time with a promised blessing. The question that needs to be asked, however, is how truly strong was Abraham's faith? In the text that we're about to look at, we're going to find out. What we're going to witness is that until we're able to give up everything that

> Until we're able to give up everything that we are and have to the Lord, we cannot truly say we have a faith in God.

we are and have to the Lord, we cannot truly say we have a faith in God.

God will test our faith by challenging us with that to which we most cling. We see it with Abraham.

> "Some time later God tested Abraham. He said to him, 'Abraham!' 'Here I am,' he replied. Then God said, 'Take your son, your only son, Isaac, whom you love, and go to the region of Moriah. Sacrifice him there as a burnt offering on one of the mountains I will tell you about.'"[6]

The text doesn't give Abraham's immediate reaction to God's command. But I know how I would have reacted if God came to me with the same request. Looking at a beloved picture of my daughter Bethany, I would have been shocked and repulsed. Maybe Abraham had some doubts that this was from the Lord. Perhaps he said to himself, "God surely wouldn't want me to behave like my Canaanite neighbors who regularly sacrifice their own children to false gods. My God wouldn't ask me to do such a thing because it would be a sin."

Secondly, he may have questioned the logic of the request. "God told me he would make me a mighty nation through this son. How can he accomplish his own will when he wants me to kill Isaac? It doesn't make sense."

---

[6] Genesis 22:1-2 NIV

Finally, he may have thought he got the request confused. "God had me send one son away. Why would he want me to give up the only one I have left?"

Abraham could have, or maybe should have, challenged God for any of these reasons, and maybe a dozen others. But he didn't. In fact, his only response to God's call was, "Here I am," the same response the future prophets, Moses, Samuel, and Isaiah, would give. It is a reply that demonstrates complete obedience and a willingness to heed the Lord at all costs. How would you respond? When God calls you, do you respond with, "Here I am," or is it more likely, "Wait, God, I'm not sure!" Faithful obedience demands that we're ready to always answer the call and command of God.

That's what Abraham did. The patriarch responded, not with worry or anxiety, but with incredible unswerving faith. There was no hesitation in carrying out God's command. Looking at verse 3: *"Early the next morning Abraham got up and saddled his donkey."* Note that Abraham didn't procrastinate. He wasn't ambivalent. The very next day, early in the morning, he wanted to start out. The text goes on...

> *"He took with him two of his servants and his son Isaac. When he had cut enough wood for the burnt offering, he set out for the place God had told him about. On the third day Abraham looked up and saw the place in the distance. He said to his servants, 'Stay here with the donkey while I and the boy go over there. We will worship and then we will come back to you.'"*

Note the incredible faith of this man. Fully intending to sacrifice his son, he brings enough wood for the altar. And look at his response to the servants: *"We* [my son and I] *will worship God and then we* [my son and I] *will come back to you."*

Question: How would Abraham be able to bring Isaac back to his servants if he was fully intending to sacrifice the boy? *Answer*: It's because Abraham fully believed that God would raise his son back from the dead. Forget faith healing – this guy believed that God would resurrect his boy! The text continues...

> *"Abraham took the wood for the burnt offering and placed it on his son Isaac, and he himself carried the fire and the knife. As the two of them went on together, Isaac spoke up and said to his father Abraham, 'Father?'*
>
> *'Yes, my son?' Abraham replied.*
>
> *'The fire and wood are here,' Isaac said, 'but where is the lamb for the burnt offering?'*
>
> *Abraham answered, 'God himself will provide the lamb for the burnt offering, my son.' And the two of them went on together."*[7]

It is interesting that the first person to reply in this narrative is Isaac. The young man asked the logical question, "Father, if we're here to sacrifice to the Lord, where is the lamb for the burnt offering?" The answer Abraham gave tells us, once again, of his incredible faith in God. "God himself will provide the lamb." God, the *provider*. He is *Jehovah Jireh, the God who provides*. Abraham understood the true nature of faith, which is the answer for all of our doubts. When things don't seem to make sense, when life throws us

---
[7] Genesis 22:6-8 NIV

a curve ball and we don't know how to respond, the key is that God will provide the answer. Abraham had a silent confidence that God had his best interest at hand. The text continues: *"When they reached the place God had told him about, Abraham built an altar there and arranged the wood on it. He bound his son Isaac and laid him on the altar, on top of the wood."*[8]

When I first read the above text, I thought that Isaac had little faith because Abraham had to bind him down to keep him on the altar. But then I thought about it, "Wait, a minute, Isaac is a strapping teenage boy, and Abraham is over 100 years old." It would be like a wrestling match between a high school varsity tackle and his grandfather who is on Social Security. If Isaac wanted to overpower the old man, he could have done it at any time. Instead, he obediently followed his father's instructions and, after carrying the wood to the altar, voluntarily placed himself upon it. Now it was up to Abraham to follow through in obedience...

> *"Then* [Abraham] *reached out his hand and took the knife to slay his son. But the angel of the LORD called out to him from heaven, 'Abraham! Abraham!'*
>
> *'Here I am,'* he replied. (Once again we witness that Abraham responded in obedience.)
>
> *'Do not lay a hand on the boy,'* he said. *'Do not do anything to him. Now I know that you fear God, because you have not withheld from me your son, your only son.'"*[9]

---

[8] Genesis 22:9 NIV
[9] Genesis 22:10-12 NIV

God commanded Abraham to give a sacrifice that day, and the Lord himself provided an alternative to the son. A ram was found caught in a thicket and Abraham used it as an offering to the Lord. Then the Angel of the Lord gave Abraham this blessing:

> *"I swear by myself, declares the LORD, that because you have done this and have not withheld your son, your only son, I will surely bless you and make your descendants as numerous as the stars in the sky and as the sand on the seashore. Your descendants will take possession of the cities of their enemies, and through your offspring all nations on earth will be blessed, because you have obeyed me."*[10]

As we sit back and reflect upon this incredible account, we realize that we've witnessed a vivid illustration of faith in action. Abraham has been a role model in how to live in uncompromising obedience to God. What can we take away from this story that will enable us to change how we live? I think we learn three truths:

Three Truths about Uncompromising Obedience

1. True worship is demonstrated in total *surrender* to God.

Throughout the narrative, we feel tension because we know that, because of his merciful nature, God never intended Isaac to be sacrificed. From a heavenly perspective, we know it is a test of absolute obedience. But Abraham

---
[10] Genesis 22:16-18 NIV

didn't know it was a test. His sole purpose in life was to worship this God who, up until this point, had been completely faithful to him. Sometimes we think that worship is about attending church Sunday mornings or singing praise songs during the service. That's only part of worship.

True worship is fearing and revering the God of the universe. True worship in the Lord means that you are willing to surrender everything you have and are to God. Note that when Abraham got his son back, he didn't say, "Whew! Okay, let's go back down the mountain." No, first he sacrificed. He gave thanks. He worshiped Yahweh. And when we worship the Lord, we need to do the same. We need to recognize that God is in control and, that for us to love him, we must surrender everything to him – our spouses, our children, our parents, our homes, our jobs, our lives. It all belongs to God, and he can do whatever he wants with it.

> **True worship is fearing and revering the God of the universe. True worship in the Lord means that you are willing to surrender everything you have and are to God.**

This truth of total surrender to God's will reminds me of the story of a little girl who was frightened of the lightening flashes and the pealing thunder as she was about to go to bed. Suddenly the lights went out, and her parents immediately came into her room to provide comfort. They encouraged her to say her prayers.

"Dear God, I hope it doesn't thunder and I hope the lights don't go out," she prayed. But after a brief pause she added, "But I thought it over, and you can do whatever you want. In Jesus name, Amen."

Abraham had this attitude toward God. He truly worshiped the Lord by surrendering all to him. And likewise, we need to be able to give everything over to the Lord. Not our will, but his be done. True worship means complete surrender.

2. True faith manifests itself in complete *trust* of God.

Abraham was tested by God because he wanted to know if Abraham would be willing to give up that which was most precious to him. The challenge for us as Christ-followers is we are willing to only partly trust God, but what is it that we're not willing to give completely over to Him?

I recall vividly the day that God called me into full-time ministry. I also remember telling him subsequent to that meeting that I was willing to fulfill that call and become a pastor, but I would not be open to becoming a missionary. I told him that I would be willing to pastor in the San Francisco Bay Area, but I wouldn't move away from my family and friends in Northern California.

We see from the life of Abraham that partial-trust isn't trust at all. For us who give stipulations on how far we'll go with God, partial trust is merely convenience. God expects and deserves our full trust.

> **We see from the life of Abraham that partial-trust isn't trust at all. For us who give stipulations on how far we'll go with God, partial trust is merely convenience.**

A man was walking along a narrow path along mountainous terrain, not paying much attention to where he was going. Suddenly, he slipped over the edge of a cliff. As he fell, he grabbed a branch growing from a protruding cleft. Realizing that he couldn't hang on for very long, he called for help.

    Man: Help! Is anybody up there?

    Voice: Yes, I'm here!

    Man: Who are you?

    Voice: It's the Lord.

    Man: Thank you, Lord! Please save me.

    Voice: Do you trust me?

    Man: I trust you completely, Lord.

    Voice: Good. Let go of the branch.

    Man: What???

    Voice: I said, "Let go of the branch."

    Man: Is anybody else up there? Help, save me!

Many times we're just like this man in that we set parameters on how far we'll trust God with our lives. We trust him when we want to get pregnant, but won't trust him if the fetus is diagnosed with Down syndrome. We'll trust him to help us find a job, but not in a field that will pay us less than we expect in salary. We'll trust him with helping us find a mate, but only if he or she is exactly the way we think he/she should be, not what God wants him or her to be. And God is telling us that partial faith isn't faith at all. Faith requires that we trust him completely.

3. **True hope believes that the Lord will *provide* for all of my needs.**

I praise the Lord that I have been a Christ-follower for almost three decades. Since 1983, I have endeavored to walk faithfully with the Lord. Sometimes I've been on fire for God and, at others, merely going through the motions. But in spite of my faithfulness, or lack thereof, the Father has always been faithful to me. One area that I struggled with trusting God was in the area of finding a mate. Before I married Kathy, I was previously engaged, not just once, but twice! The first time was when I was 31 and the second was at 35. In both cases, it was the woman who broke off the engagement.

Needless to say, I was deeply hurt and anxious – hurt by the rejection and anxious that I might never find a mate. But in spite of the feelings of doubt, deep down, I knew that God had been faithful to me thus far in every aspect of my life; therefore, I knew he would be faithful in finding me the perfect mate. If these past girlfriends seemed pretty good, well then the one God wanted me ultimately to be with would be incredible. And she is. Kathy has far exceeded any of my expectations for a wife and mother, and I tell her every day how much I love her and am thankful that God brought her into my life.

> **Sometimes in the midst of our trials and tests, the only thing we can cling to is the hope that God will provide for all our needs.**

Sometimes in the midst of our trials and tests, the only thing we can cling to is the hope that God will provide for all our needs. That's not easy when you've been laid off and see no other job opportunities in sight. That's hard, when as a single, you've just celebrated your 40th birthday and there's no potential mate in sight. That's difficult when you've been diagnosed with inoperable cancer. And it seems unachievable when, like Abraham, God presents you with a truly impossible situation. But if this incident tells us anything, it's that we have a God who overcomes the impossible. He is Jehovah Jireh, the God who provides.

Whatever your level of faith is today, pray that God would increase what amount you have so that, when tested, you might witness and enjoy God's incredible blessing!

Taking Time to Get Real

Heart-to-Heart

Take some time to reflect upon God's faithfulness in your life. As you pray, ask the Lord to reveal what area, incident, person, and/or event is challenging you to fully trust him? Take the time to ask the Holy Spirit to increase your faith and decrease your doubt.

Questions for Discussion

- When you read the daily news, what captures your attention the most? What is it about this topic that intrigues you?

- What is your greatest challenge right now in trusting God? Why has it been so difficult?

- All of us have some areas of our lives that have not been totally surrendered to the Lord. What is that area and why has it been so difficult to give up?

- Ask a close Christian friend and/or mentor what area of your life demonstrates only a partial trust in God. Do you agree or disagree? Why or why not?

- What is your greatest need right now? What is your greatest want right now? Do you believe God will provide it for you, and if so, how?

Memory Verse: Hebrews 11:17-19

By faith Abraham, when God tested him, offered Isaac as a sacrifice. He who had received the promises was about to sacrifice his one and only son, even though God had said to him, "It is through Isaac that your offspring will be reckoned." Abraham reasoned that God could raise the dead, and figuratively speaking, he did receive Isaac back from death.

Heartwork

On a sheet of paper, make a line down the center. On the left side, write as many personal examples as you can of how God has been completely faithful to you. On the right, write down the incidences where you have demonstrated trust in him when the circumstances seemed nearly impossible. What do you learn from this exercise about faith, trust, and obedience?

Sarah

Taking Matters into My Own Hands
Genesis 16:1-16

I've had the privilege of leading hundreds of Bible studies in my ministry. One of my favorite formats is Question and Answer. In this type of study, members of the class are allowed to ask any type of question they want. In my many years of ministry, I've been asked a lot of interesting questions. There are, of course, the standard ones: Did Adam have a navel? Did Cain marry his sister? Where do dinosaurs fit into the creation story? But then, there are more difficult ones: How can God predestine us for salvation and yet we have the free will to choose him? There are a lot of questions, some a little quirky, but they're interesting nonetheless. Do you know what question is the most frequently asked of all? It's this: *How do I find God's will for my life?*

> *How do I find God's will for my life?*

Perhaps it's the question you have on your mind right now. You've struggled in your faith because the answer doesn't seem readily transparent. It's not like you can take your Bible, randomly open it up, stick your finger on a page, and read God's will for your life.

By the way, if that is how you sometimes try to discern God's will, you're asking for trouble. Taking Scripture out of context is not only wrong, it's dangerous. It can lead to various humorous situations, like the time our church had a short-term mission trip to Mexico. Someone posted on the outside of one of the port-o-lets: "What you do, do it quickly." Now, that's what I call true bathroom humor! These words were spoken to Judas by the Lord when he was ready to betray him. Now change the scenario — imagine you're depressed to the point of suicide and looking for an answer from God. You open your Bible randomly and your finger comes to this very same passage: "What you do, do it quickly!" Very dangerous!

Finding and fulfilling God's specific will for your life is difficult. Does the Lord want you to move away for college or stay at home? Does he want you to buy a house right here, or does he want you to take a job across the country? Are you to marry this person or wait for another? Does the Lord want you to super-size your meal? (Your primary care physician can answer that one...No!) As a pastor, many in my congregation have asked me these very same questions, and I can honestly say that I don't know God's will in these particular matters...he didn't tell me and, evidently, he didn't tell them either.

A Desire for Direct Revelation

Wouldn't it be great if, as in the days of old, God spoke to us and just simply told us what he wanted us to do? For example, we saw in the last chapter how God talked to

Abram (his original name before God changed it to Abraham):

> "The LORD had said to Abram, 'Leave your country, your people and your father's household and go to the land I will show you. I will make you into a great nation and I will bless you; I will make your name great, and you will be a blessing.'"[11]

We wish God would be so direct with us. Scripture tells us that Abram did obey the Lord's command and took his nephew Lot with him to the land of Canaan. In this Promised Land, Abram let his nephew have first choice on which land he wanted to settle, and Lot chose the plains of Jordan. Abram took the leftovers, the land of Canaan. Note that he didn't force his way into getting what he thought was the best, but rather, took God at his promise, and the Lord affirmed that he made the right choice.

> "The LORD said to Abram after Lot had parted from him, 'Lift up your eyes from where you are and look north and south, east and west. All the land that you see I will give to you and your offspring forever. I will make your offspring like the dust of the earth, so that if anyone could count the dust, then your offspring could be counted.'"[12]

In football lingo, Abram got an "audible" from God. "I want you to have this land, and I'll give you the offspring to

---

[11] Genesis 12:1-2 NIV
[12] Genesis 13:14-16 NIV

populate it." The only problem from a human standpoint was that Abram's wife Sarai (later known as Sarah) was biologically unable to have children. In the story of Sarai and her maidservant Hagar, who comes into the picture later, we're going to learn that fulfilling God's will is not just a matter of the *outcome*, but also is dependent upon the *process*. It may take some time to fulfill God's sovereign will.

> Fulfilling God's will is not just a matter of the *outcome*, but also is dependent upon the *process*.

My grandmother, a devout believer, who came to the Lord through missionaries who shared Christ with her in China, prayed daily for over two decades before she saw me become a Christian at 21. If you're mathematically challenged, that's over 7,500 times! I thank the Lord he chose me to be his son, but I believe that the process of my spiritual adoption was just as important as the result. God cared that my grandmother was fervent in her prayers for my salvation as he was for my salvation.

Perhaps there's someone in your life that you've been praying for years to be healed, and God in his infinite wisdom does not allow instantaneous healing, but instead has allowed for a more gradual process of restoration. Or you anxiously desire to get married as soon as possible, but for some reason, God seems to be pushing the wedding day out farther than you expect or want. For God, the timing is as important as the outcome in regard to his will. It's not just about a person becoming a Christian, or being healed, or getting married that's important to God; he's also concerned with the process, where growth and development are experienced.

The Need for Speed

Americans, for the most part, are a very impatient people. Just think of how we approach food. We were the inventors of fast food.[13] And though Cup Noodles™ was created in Japan in 1958, American collegians have made it a staple for dorm-life living for half a century.

While watching a microwave oven do its thing with a bag of popcorn, I once told a young person that we used to make popcorn the old-fashioned way. He thought I meant using an airless popper, but I meant oil in a pot. Parents opt out of cooking at home and, instead, feed little Johnny his weekly Happy Meal which, of course, they pick up at the drive-through window. The multitude's mantra reverberates across the land: "We want it, and we want it now!" For the most part, that shouldn't be a problem, if you want to live your life that way. But sometimes when it comes to fulfilling God's will, we cut a few corners in trying to speed things up. We add a little *human* intervention to circumvent *divine* intervention when it seems like the Lord Almighty isn't holding up his end of the bargain.

> We add a little *human* intervention to circumvent *divine* intervention when it seems like the Lord Almighty isn't holding up his end of the bargain.

It reminds me of what was said at one of my church's youth graduation events. A parent gave advice to his graduating teenager: "Do your best, and give God the rest."

---

[13] Unlike what you might believe, the first fast food hamburger restaurant was not McDonalds, but rather, Whitecastle in Wichita, Kansas, 1916.

Sounds good, doesn't it? Put out your best effort, and then when all else fails, rely on God. I've seen this philosophy lived out in the church all the time.

A Christian couple, desiring to have children, uses fertility drugs. They are shocked when they find out the wife is carrying quintuplets. The doctor says the best chance for the survivability of the children is selective abortion. What should they do? What is God's will and how do they go about fulfilling it?

A young man applies for college and is accepted to both the local state university and an Ivy League school. Where should he go? What is God's will and how does he go about fulfilling it?

A young woman just finishing her studies at UCLA is offered employment in Nome, Alaska. Should she stay put in Southern California and hope to find a better offer, or should she take the employment opportunity in the frozen tundra of America's last frontier? What is God's will and how does she go about fulfilling it?

A young, single pastor finds the metro-Phoenix area, in which he ministers, to be a "desert" in more ways than one. He has a great church, but realizes that it seems like rather slim pickin's when it comes to available women. On the other hand, California, from which he has roots, seems to be busting at the seams with single females. Should he move or stay? What is God's will for his marital status and how does he go about fulfilling it?

Taking Matters into Your Own Hands

In a way, that's the situation we have with Abram's wife, Sarai. And the objective of this chapter is to learn about fulfilling God's will by looking at her and her maidservant Hagar. Let's begin by pondering the situation: *"Now Sarai, Abram's wife, had borne him no children."*[14]

Abram and Sarai left Ur while they were very old. The reason she couldn't have children wasn't because she was beyond child-bearing years, but rather, because she was barren. It was physically impossible for her to have children. Yet she, no doubt, remembered God's promise that he would make her husband the father of a great nation. Ten more years had passed in this new land, her biological clock seeming to come to a standstill. As the months passed on, she must have questioned when and how God was going to keep his promise. So she decided to take matters into her own hands...

> *"But she [Sarai] had an Egyptian maidservant named Hagar; so she said to Abram, 'The LORD has kept me from having children. Go, sleep with my maidservant; perhaps I can build a family through her.' Abram agreed to what Sarai said. So after Abram had been living in Canaan ten years, Sarai his wife took her Egyptian maidservant Hagar and gave her to her husband to be his wife. He slept with Hagar, and she conceived."*[15]

---

[14] Genesis 16:1 NIV
[15] Genesis 16:1b-4a NIV

This servant, Hagar, was an Egyptian, not one of their own people. The legal custom of that day was that a wife could give her husband her maidservant, and the child born of that union would belong to that wife. If the man adopted the son, he would have all the legal rights afforded to him. Even though this decision by Sarai seemed to make sense, this was not God's way of fulfilling his promise. We see this in an interesting similarity between Genesis 3, the fall of man, and Genesis 16:2-3:

> 16:2a "So she [Sarai] said to..."
> 3:2 "The woman [Eve] said to..."
>
> 16:2b "Abram agreed to what Sarai said."
> 3:17 "You [Adam] listened to your wife."
>
> 16:3a "Sarah...took"
> 3:6a "She [Eve] took some..."
>
> 16:3b "And she [Sarai] gave her to her husband"
> 3:6b "She [Eve] also gave some to her husband."

The fall of mankind came about because Eve fell to the temptation put out by the serpent. She sought wisdom, she sought to be like God, and she circumvented God's perfect plan for her and Adam's lives. Likewise, Sarai tried to circumvent God's process and sought to carry out the Lord's will her way. Sarai wanted to fulfill a *divine* promise by supplying it with a *human* solution. And unlike what Frank

> **Sarai wanted to fulfill a *divine* promise by supplying it with a *human* solution.**

Sinatra sings, God wants it his way, not my way. And when we try to do it our way, we end up with a lot of hurt. Look at the results:

> *"When she [Hagar] knew she was pregnant, she began to despise her mistress. Then Sarai said to Abram, 'You are responsible for the wrong I am suffering. I put my servant in your arms, and now that she knows she is pregnant, she despises me. May the LORD judge between you and me.'*
>
> *'Your servant is in your hands,' Abram said. 'Do with her whatever you think best.' Then Sarai mistreated Hagar; so she fled from her."*[16]

Everyone ended up hurt in this situation. Let's first look at Hagar. The text says she *despised* her mistress. That Hebrew word means "to curse." We can certainly sympathize with her situation because she was a slave with very little rights and was being forced to have sexual relations with a man. But in the end, Hagar gave her master what his wife could not, and this led Hagar to be filled with pride, demonstrated by showing disdain for her mistress.

Sarai, too, was affected by her decision. When things don't go the way we plan, what we usually end up doing is blaming others. And that's what we see with Sarai. She ordered her husband to sleep with that woman and then, when the results turned out the way she wanted, she had the audacity to blame Abram for what happened.

Finally, Abram was affected as well. Being weak-willed and wife-beaten, did he stand up to Sarai? No, like Adam

---

[16] Genesis 16:4-6 NIV

before him, he simply went along with his wife's bad advice. He didn't want to deal with the issue, so he abdicated the authority that God gave him as a husband. (And frankly, as a pastor, I've seen a little too much of this within Christian families.) So the result is that Sarai had the full right to mistreat her slave. That same word is used of the Egyptians in how they would later mistreat the Jews in their land. Hagar, not being able to take the harsh treatment, fled. But God was with her.

> *"The angel of the LORD found Hagar near a spring in the desert; it was the spring that is beside the road to Shur. And he said, 'Hagar, servant of Sarai, where have you come from, and where are you going?' 'I'm running away from my mistress Sarai,' she answered. Then the angel of the LORD told her, 'Go back to your mistress and submit to her.' The angel added, 'I will so increase your descendants that they will be too numerous to count.'"*[17]

A Call to Obedience

Within this passage, we see a familiar pattern that God desires of us when we seek to fulfill his will. The first is a call to *obedience*. Note that the Lord said to Hagar through his angel in verse 9, *"Go back to your mistress and submit to her."* Now put yourself in this slave's place. You've been obedient, you did the right thing. You submitted to your master and to his demanding wife, and you bless them with

---

[17] Genesis 16:7-10 NIV

a child, *your* child, that you willingly give up. In return for your obedience, you get beaten up, yelled at, and kicked out.

All of us would be in agreement that you have every right to say, "Forget it." You have every right to say, like Hagar, "I want to go back to my place of security, back on the road to Shur toward Egypt." That's the obvious decision to make. That's the alternative that makes the most sense. You may be a wife who feels like Hagar in your relationship to your husband. You may be a child who feels like Hagar in relationship to your parents, who act like Sarai. You may be an employee who feels like Hagar when you have a boss who acts like Sarai. The rational, common-sense, expected response to such treatment is to flee. But sometimes God has a different plan. Instead, he might want you to stay and take the heat. He wants you to stick it out rather than flee.

God Desires to Bless

So the first action we need to take is to obey God. But the second aspect of fulfilling God's will is seen in the Lord's promise. He says if you obey, then he will *bless* you. For the people of the Old Testament, there were two types of blessings – prosperity and posterity. Prosperity was measured in the attainment of land, which represented wealth. Posterity was achieved through the bearing of many children. In this case, God told Hagar to obey him and go back and submit to her mistress, and he would bless her posterity by making her descendents too numerous to count.

In addition, through the Angel of the Lord, God reaffirmed that he would be with Hagar:

> "The angel of the LORD also said to her: 'You are now with child and you will have a son. You shall name him Ishmael, for the LORD has heard of your misery. He will be a wild donkey of a man; his hand will be against everyone and everyone's hand against him, and he will live in hostility toward all his brothers.'
>
> She gave this name to the LORD who spoke to her: 'You are the God who sees me,' for she said, 'I have now seen the One who sees me.' That is why the well was called Beer Lahai Roi; it is still there, between Kadesh and Bered.
>
> So Hagar bore Abram a son, and Abram gave the name Ishmael to the son she had borne. Abram was eighty-six years old when Hagar bore him Ishmael."[18]

There are two ways that God confirmed that he was with Hagar the slave. First, he said to name the child Ishmael, which means, "God has heard." Sometimes in the midst of our troubles, we call out, thinking no one hears. But God always hears. He hears when no one else seems to be listening, when life seems unbearable and hopeless. He'll never leave us; he'll never forsake us. But there's another way that confirmed that God was with Hagar. Remember, Hagar was a pagan – she didn't know Yahweh, the God of Abram. So after hearing

---
[18] Genesis 16:11-16 NIV

him, she dedicated the well she rested at as Beer Lahai Roi, which means "the God who sees me." When you feel all alone and no one is around, God is there. He sees your pain; he hears your pain. He's always there for you. Hagar obeyed God and submitted to her mistress. And God fulfilled his will by blessing her.

As we come to the end of the chapter, I think there are five lessons that we can learn from our main characters in this drama.

Lessons to Learn from Sarai and Hagar

1. The fulfillment of God's promise may take *patient waiting*.

Sarai was 65 and barren, but she knew that God had promised to bless her and Abram with children. Instead of taking matters into her own hands, she should have inquired of the Lord. She should have called out to Him. She should have prayed to God for guidance. But she didn't. She did it her way and paid the consequences.

Sometimes we do the same thing. We might think that God wants us to have certain ministries involved in evangelism or missions, or fellowship development, or worship, and we think, "Well, let's get cracking." And we begin to build these ministries on our own ability and time frame, rather than waiting for God to bless us in his way.

My church learned that lesson the hard way in acquiring new property. Our senior pastor and I first came across a church that was selling their property, and we believed that this was the Promised Land for us. At first, we tried to push it on our congregation, and it almost backfired. Ultimately, it turned out to be God's will for us to have this property, but he wanted us to learn some lessons along the way: trusting in the Lord, patience with naysayers, and building unity.

Sometimes God calls for us to be patient, to wait for him to fulfill his will.

2. *Passivity* **is not the same as** *patience.*

Some would say, "Well then, rather than move forward, we should wait on all things. We don't do anything; just go with the flow." But what we learn from Abram's reaction to Sarai's demands is that *passivity* is not the same as *patience*. God doesn't want us to do our best and give him the rest. But he doesn't want us to just sit back and let things happen either. Again, to seek God's will, we need to discern what he wants us to do.

The best way to find out if God is calling you to a teaching ministry is not to sit back and wait for someone to ask you to teach a Bible Study; rather, we need to volunteer and seek out the opportunity. The best way to find out if God might be calling you to full time ministry is not to just keep going on with your life as it's always been – same old job, same old house payment, same old routine – instead, seek out opportunities to test if full-time ministry is from God. Talk to your pastor or church leader about service. Passivity is not the same as patience.

3. God is not a respecter of *culture*.

Sometimes as Americans, we get tunnel vision about how God works and through whom He is doing his will. And we forget that the world is bigger than the United States and his kingdom will be populated by more than Americans. God blessed Hagar, an Egyptian pagan. Why would he do that? We don't know why. But what it tells us is that God is not a respecter of race or culture. He loves all people. Of course, we should know that already since Jesus proclaimed that, *"God so loved the world that he gave his only begotten son so that whoever believes in him would not perish, but have everlasting life."*[19]

And in regard to this salvation that God offers, the Apostle Peter in his little letter said, *"The Lord is not slow in keeping his promise, as some understand slowness. He is patient with you, not wanting anyone to perish, but everyone to come to repentance."*[20]

All churches carry a unique identity. It's something from which we should not shy away or be ashamed. But God never intended for the church to be an exclusive club. If it's God's will that none should perish, who are we to turn away from the doors of the our church some who don't fit our particular demographic or culture?

May I be blunt in suggesting that most Christ-followers are totally clueless when it comes to the bias, prejudices, and preconceived notions we have about others, even and especially within the Christian community. I am not in a position to judge you or your church.

---

[19] John 3:16 NIV
[20] 2 Peter 3:8-9 NIV

As a pastor in a bi-cultural Chinese church, we have our prejudices, too. We had an Anglo family come visit our church. They had an opportunity to go overseas to China with the husband's company. They looked at this as a God-given opportunity for evangelism, so they left their home church and joined our church. The husband once told me, however, that he would be approached on occasion by the Chinese-speaking congregants, who would directly ask, "Why are you coming to this church?" The implication was that they were not Chinese. Praise God that they weren't offended. They have come to love and embrace the Chinese culture.

Our cultural roots are so ingrained that we don't even realize that it defines what we think is appropriate and inappropriate, what is normal and what is strange. I challenge you to take one Sunday and visit a church of a different ethnic background or, if you're younger, go to a church primarily filled with Senior citizens. Or vice-versa, if you're older, go to a less traditional church. If you're from the city, attend a rural church. And if you are able, I strongly encourage you to go on an international short-term mission not only to serve, but just as importantly, to learn. Yes, you may do some good for the people you serve, but honestly, it will do you more good to broaden your perspective on what God's kingdom is really all about. You will have a paradigm shift in your faith and understand that God is not a respecter of culture. He loves everyone and he loves different kinds of worship.

4. **God *hears* and *sees* our misery.**

When we think of our friends or family, we think of those who love us unconditionally. But as good as their love is it can never be perfect. Many of you are frustrated with your small group, the ministry in which you serve, or with the leadership of your church. You feel as if no one understands or cares about your issues or struggles. The wonderful truth about our faith is that, when no one else seems to notice, your Heavenly Father always hears and sees your misery. He will never leave you. He will never forget you. He took time out of his busy schedule to minister to a poor pagan slave girl because he loved her. And he loves you, too. God hears and sees your misery.

5. **Taking matters into our own hands can cause things to become *worse*.**

Sarai, in her best understanding, sought to fulfill God's will. But she did it through her own way and by her own means, and the result was that, rather than being a blessing, it complicated her life. The historical epilogue to this whole ordeal is that her sin caused the origination of the Ishmaelites, the children of Ishmael, who was the son of Hagar. And just as God had promised, they became a wild donkey of a people, and their hand was against everyone, including themselves. They hated everyone. But most of all, they hated the children of Abram's other son, a son born out of promise, Isaac.

The Ishmaelites were children of Abram. But instead of following the faith of Isaac, Judaism, they eventually would follow the faith of one of their own prophets, Mohammed. If you haven't figured it out yet, the Ishmaelites are the Arabs. The fighting that has continued from centuries in the past to the present day – and probably well into the future in the Middle East – the division between Palestinians and Jews, the hatred of Arabs for the Israelites, the killing, the terrorist bombings, the murders, 9/11, can all be traced back to Sarai's desire to fulfill God's plan by her own means.

Hagar was blessed. Ishmael was blessed. But Sarai's intervention cost her future son, Isaac, grief. Let's learn from Sarai. Let's pursue God's will, but let's do it on God's time table, not our own. Let's do it God's way, not our own. Let's be people of patience. Obey, submit, be blessed.

Taking Time to Get Real

Heart-to-Heart

Reflect at this time and ponder how you've lived your life. Do you tend to rely on your own abilities, intelligence, and means to get ahead in life, or have you trusted the Lord in every aspect of living? Pray and ask the Lord to give you understanding where you need to let go, and let God take control.

Questions for Discussion

- Can you think of any examples in your life where you believed God not only cared about what happened in your life, but also how it happened? What were they and how do you think God used the process to grow your faith?

- Can you recall some specific instances where you might have deprived yourself of blessings because you did it your way instead of God's way? What were the results and what could have been had following God's path?

- Can you describe times where you actually were disobedient to God in doing things your way? Did God discipline you? If so, how?

- Can you recall times when you struggled in your life and God eventually blessed your patience in trusting him? What happened? Was it worth the wait?

- Has God placed you in situations which tested your comfort level within your own culture? What did you learn about the other way people do things? How did this change the way you think about others in the way they worship God?

Memory Verse: Proverbs 3:5-8

Trust in the Lord with all your heart and lean not on your own understanding; in all your ways acknowledge him, and he will make your paths straight. Do not be wise in your own eyes; fear the Lord and shun evil. This will bring health to your body and nourishment to your bones.

Heartwork

Make the intention that you will visit another church within the next few weeks that is culturally different than your home church. Pray about what it is the Lord wants you to learn. Be open-minded and non-judgmental about what you experience. You will not be comfortable, but through your discomfort, God will teach you something about his children. Share what you experienced with others in your church.

Elizabeth

Embracing a Second-Fiddle Attitude
Luke 1

My wife and I are blessed (or cursed, depending upon your perspective) with being the eldest among three siblings in each of our respective families. Those who aren't the oldest probably look, with envy, to the senior sibling as the one with all the privileges, being the measuring stick for all following children to emulate.

For example, in my freshman year of high school English, my teacher thought my poem was so good that he read it aloud to the rest of the class which, though embarrassing at the time, in hindsight was really an honor. My brother Alan took the same class and had the same teacher two years later. I was surprised to find out that the teacher kept a copy of the poem and read it in my brother's class. The teacher was glancing at Alan the whole time, and my brother knew the expectation was that he should produce something of similar quality. Not likely!

The same thing happened to Alan three years later in honors biology. I was "Biology Student of the Year" two years previous, and the teacher expected similar results from my brother. He didn't even come close, which is not to say that Alan's a dummy. Actually he's very intelligent, but he's just not book smart. The cold reality is that Alan was never able to measure up to me scholastically, but in matters related to sports, he left me in the dust. While I was poring over books in the school library, he was playing varsity tennis and badminton.

Two years later, my younger sister followed my brother. Dina is one of those types of people you love to hate because she excels at everything. She was a synchronized swimmer and was on both the varsity swimming and badminton teams. In addition, she was an honors student and graduated one position higher than me in her class. As a graduate of Cal (UC Berkeley) with a Master's in Public Health, to this day, she likes to rib me that, as a Cal-State University, Hayward (now called Cal-State University, East Bay), alumnus, it would take me at least four more degrees to equal what she's accomplished.

Being Number One

Among your siblings, it might have been or is the same way: you excel in certain areas over them, and they surpass you in others. There can only be one number one. We can't all be the best. Just ask Venus or Serena Williams, or Eli or Payton Manning; there's only one number one.

Nobody wants to take second place – we want the blue ribbon. Any avid sports fan can tell you in any given year who won the NCAA finals, the Super Bowl, or the World Series. But they will have a more difficult time recalling who the champions beat. A political junkie can give the name of the last twenty presidents, but they will be harder pressed to name their defeated opponents. Nobody remembers the runner up because being number two is for losers.

In fact, it was the famed football coach Vince Lombardi who once said, "Show me a good loser, and I'll show you a loser." That sounds harsh, especially during these times, when we live in a culture that desires not to denigrate by comparing the sub-par or average individual to the cream of the crop. We don't want to diminish anyone's self-worth. Back in the '70s when I was in high school, we had what was called the *Herculean Award*, which was given to varsity athletes who lettered at least seven times. Those plaques were proudly displayed in our school gym. I was told by a friend, who received the Herculean Award, that all of those plaques have since been taken down. He found his with his younger sister's in the garbage bins. The reason for their removal was because the school didn't want to humiliate those students who didn't perform at such a high level.

> "Show me a good loser, and I'll show you a loser."

For most of us, the actions of my school may seem kind of silly, in light of the harsh reality of life, where every person is compared to someone else. We want to know where we stand in relation to the classmate sitting next to us. (That's why we get letter grades in public schools.) We aspire to the top position, not second best. We are inquisitive with those surveys of top schools in the nation. We want our kid playing first string on the football team, not warming the bench. We buy front row seats to the musical to hear the headliner, not the understudy.

The great conductor Leonard Bernstein had something to say about being second best. When asked, "What is the most difficult instrument to play?" He responded, with a sly grin, "Second fiddle. I can get plenty of first violinists, but to find one who plays second violin with as much enthusiasm, or second French horn or second flute, now that's a problem. And yet if no one plays second, we have no harmony."

Bernstein is right. No one wants to play second fiddle; and yet in this chapter, we're going to be introduced to a woman who fulfilled the understudy role with enthusiasm and gusto. Let's look at her story:

> *"In the time of Herod king of Judea there was a priest named Zechariah, who belonged to the priestly division of Abijah; his wife Elizabeth was also a descendant of Aaron. Both of them were upright in the sight of God, observing all the Lord's commandments and regulations blamelessly. But they had no children, because Elizabeth was barren; and they were both well along in years."*[21]

About Elizabeth

The woman we'll be looking at in this chapter is Elizabeth. Her husband Zechariah was a priest, and both were descendents of Aaron, the priest. We find out that they were known for their good character and righteousness before God. Zechariah, as a priest, was well respected by the people. It is unfortunate, however, that they had no children, for Elizabeth was unable to conceive, and now they were well on in years. In that culture, not being able to have children was a sign of shame. The text continues...

---

[21] Luke 1:5-7 NIV

> "*Once when Zechariah's division was on duty and he was serving as priest before God, he was chosen by lot, according to the custom of the priesthood, to go into the temple of the Lord and burn incense. And when the time for the burning of incense came, all the assembled worshipers were praying outside. Then an angel of the Lord appeared to him, standing at the right side of the altar of incense. When Zechariah saw him, he was startled and was gripped with fear.*"[22]

We learn from the above text that Zechariah was performing his ceremonial duties with his division of twenty-four priests. In those days, each division would serve two times a year for one week. Because of the large number of priests, they drew lots to offer the incense, and in this particular instance, it fell upon Zechariah. This was an extraordinary blessing for this righteous man because he might only have this one chance for his entire life to serve the Lord in this particular manner. When we get that rare chance to do something this spectacular, sometimes we chalk it up to dumb luck – and perhaps it may have seemed that way for Zechariah. But it didn't come about by random fate; God used this opportunity to bring Zechariah a message of blessing through the angel Gabriel: "*But the angel said to him: 'Do not be afraid, Zechariah; your prayer has been heard. Your wife Elizabeth will bear you a son, and you are to give him the name John.'*"[23]

---

[22] Luke 1:8-12 NIV
[23] Luke 1:13 NIV

The angel then listed five attributes with which this special son would be endowed:
1. He would be a joy and delight to his parents.
2. He would be great in the sight of God.
3. He was never to drink alcohol (he was called to be a Nazirite, chosen especially to serve God in the same manner as Samuel the prophet, and Samson the judge).
4. He would be filled with the Holy Spirit from birth.
5. He was to bring back his people to God by way of being a sign-post/guide to the promised Messiah.

> **If we could know ahead of time that our children will be walking closely with God, it would take away a lot of our concern.**

At night, sometimes I'll peer through the door at my young daughters, Bethany and Rebekah, while they're asleep. During those times, I've often wondered what they'll be like when they're older. If I could know ahead of time that they'd be walking closely with God, it would take away a lot of my concern.

The problem is we don't know the future. But what if God were to do the same for us as he did for Zechariah and provide a supernatural guest, who proclaims to us what seems to be biologically impossible? Then perhaps, we can understand why Zechariah was a little skeptical. In a rather straightforward manner, Zechariah asked the angel how this was possible: *"Give me proof that what you say is from God."* The angel responded by stating that he, himself, was from God, and that he was told to give Zechariah this good news. But since the priest didn't believe the prophecy, Zechariah would be rendered mute until the baby was born.

Imagine the crowd's reaction when Zechariah came out of the temple and was unable to speak. They realized that something supernatural had occurred. After Zechariah's service was up, he returned home and, just as the angel foretold, Elizabeth became pregnant. Now it is interesting how Elizabeth responded to this very special event. Rather than shouting it from their rooftop or boasting of her husband's work and the Lord's preference of them, she, instead, decided to keep this information to herself. She remained in seclusion for five months. And her response was telling of whom was responsible for her blessing: "*The <u>Lord</u> has done this for me. In these days he has shown his favor and taken away my disgrace among the people.*"[24]

Wouldn't it be phenomenal if we could experience the same realization of blessing that Elizabeth felt? She was so trusting of God's goodness that it overcame her natural tendency toward embarrassment and humiliation.

This is a great blessing, but God's work in the world of men is not yet complete. Seventy-five miles away in the northern region of Galilee, the angel Gabriel made another appearance:

> "*In the sixth month, God sent the angel Gabriel to Nazareth, a town in Galilee, to a virgin pledged to be married to a man named Joseph, a descendant of David. The virgin's name was Mary. The angel went to her and said, 'Greetings, you who are highly favored! The Lord is with you.'*"[25]

---

[24] Luke 1:25 NIV
[25] Luke 1:26-28 NIV

The angel told Mary that God had chosen her, a young Jewish virgin, to be with child. He was to be the anticipated Messiah, the one whose throne and kingdom will never end. Mary questioned how this would be, and Gabriel responded that the power of God would overshadow her and she would conceive. As proof, he told her of her older relative, Elizabeth, who was also with child. Unlike Zechariah, Mary believed: *"I am the Lord's servant. May it be to me as you have said."*

Mary, the mother of the future Christ, then went to meet with Elizabeth, the mother of the future Christ-pointer. In this meeting, we find that there is no competition or desire to compare children. Elizabeth understood the role that her future son was to play, and she's content to play second fiddle to Mary. So what can we learn from Elizabeth's attitude? Basically I see three truths:

1. **It is more important to be *number two* in God's kingdom than *number one* in the world's eyes.**

   "At that time Mary got ready and hurried to a town in the hill country of Judea, where she entered Zechariah's home and greeted Elizabeth. When Elizabeth heard Mary's greeting, the baby leaped in her womb, and Elizabeth was filled with the Holy Spirit. In a loud voice she exclaimed: 'Blessed are you among women, and blessed is the child you will bear! But why am I so favored, that the mother of my Lord should come to me? As soon as the sound of your greeting reached my ears, the baby in my womb leaped for

joy. *Blessed is she who has believed that what the Lord has said to her will be accomplished!'"*[26]

Elizabeth had been in seclusion. She's probably excited about this special baby boy that God had given her – a child promised to be full of the Holy Spirit even while in her womb. And then Mary, her younger relative, came walking into her home bringing the good news of her own baby, and Elizabeth could have become instantly jealous.

Fleeting thoughts of her son kowtowing to this other boy could have entered her mind. But that's not how she responded. Instead, she felt elation and joy that her son would somehow magnify Mary's son. There was no jealousy or feelings of competition. Jesus would become the valedictorian, and her son John would be the salutatorian. Jesus would someday play first-string quarterback and become the superstar. Her son John would become a second-string defensive end, a nobody. Jesus, the healer, is the Great Physician. John, the baptizer, washed people in a river. Jesus Christ, Superstar! John the Baptist, sign-post to the Savior.

Elizabeth's son would always remain in the shadow of his younger relative. It's not fun being second fiddle, but for John and his mother Elizabeth that was reality. But note that Elizabeth didn't resent it; she was overjoyed at the privilege because she had a servant's heart. She was the person that Jesus had in mind when he would later talk about a submissive spirit:

---

[26] Luke 1:39-45 NIV

> *"You know that those who are regarded as rulers of the Gentiles lord it over them, and their high officials exercise authority over them. Not so with you. Instead, whoever wants to become great among you must be your servant, and whoever wants to be first must be slave of all. For even the Son of Man did not come to be served, but to serve, and to give his life as a ransom for many."*[27]

Elizabeth understood that in God's economy, if you wanted to be great in the Kingdom, you must have a servant's heart. And she carried this attitude into her relationship with Mary.

2. It is more important to be obedient to God's *calling* than to *excel* in the world.

> *"Mary stayed with Elizabeth for about three months and then returned home. When it was time for Elizabeth to have her baby, she gave birth to a son. Her neighbors and relatives heard that the Lord had shown her great mercy, and they shared her joy. On the eighth day they came to circumcise the child, and they were going to name him after his father Zechariah, but his mother spoke up and said, 'No! He is to be called John.'*
>
> *They said to her, 'There is no one among your relatives who has that name.'*
>
> *Then they made signs to his father, to find out what he would like to name the child. He asked for a writing tablet,*

---
[27] Mark 10:42-45 NIV

and to everyone's astonishment he wrote, 'His name is John.'"[28]

Note that Zechariah and Elizabeth's friends, in love, assumed that the son would be named after the father. What does it say about us when we want our son or daughter to take our name? The answer is that there is a sense of pride in the family name. We want our children to represent us when we're long gone. We want them to do just as well, if not better than us, and carrying our name means we somehow live our lives through our kids.

> **We want our children to represent us when we're long gone.**

Perhaps that's why soccer moms and dads get so animated at games, arguing with the umps for an unfair call against their child, or yelling at the coaches for not playing their kid, or even verbally blasting their own boy for not playing as well as they think he ought to. We want them to excel in the world because they are a reflection of us, our abilities as parents to raise our children, and the values we pass on to and through them.

Somehow Elizabeth was different. Her goal was not so much that her son would be great in the world's eyes, but rather, be great in her Father's eyes. We realize this truth when this second-fiddle mom emphatically tells her friends that the boy's name is John...not Jesus, but John.

> **Elizabeth's goal was not so much that her son would be great in the world's eyes, but rather, be great in her Father's eyes.**

---

[28] Luke 1:56-62 NIV

What we name our child tells a lot about the priorities we have in regard to our children. Naming the kid Harvard, Stanford, or Cal tells others of your educational aspirations. Giving him the name Michael Jordan tells everyone how high you want him to go in basketball. Elizabeth understood that obedience to God was more important than excelling in the world. Her son's name was John, and she praised God for it.

In respect to our children's lives, we parents will be faced with decisions that have to be made with regard to priorities. No one but God can judge your choices. You desire to have your teen attend her youth camp, but wrestle with that extra week that could have been used to bone up on her studies. Your seventeen year old informs you that he wants to pursue full-time ministry, but you have your apprehension and fear. Are you open to the possibility of God's calling, or do you shut down the option right away?

You might be thinking to yourself, these kinds of decisions between the secular and sacred are rare. And yes, I do want my children to do well in school and in life, but certainly not at the cost of my children's spiritual health. That's our desire, but it's interesting that many times those intentions don't measure up to reality. In the dozen or so Youth Camps of which I've had the privilege of speaking, rarely does a young person mention their greatest challenge is maintaining a holy life. The majority will say that doing well in school and maintaining good friendships is the most important. GPAs and getting dates supersede God and discipleship.

A mother came to me many years ago complaining that her son would have been the valedictorian of his school if it wasn't for some *"Indian boy"* (which was said with a kind of disdain in her voice) with a higher GPA. I appreciated her concern for her son's standing, but I said to her, "You know, in life there can only be one number one. Everyone else is number two through number one thousand. If your child is number one, then some other child is not." I don't believe she got the point of my exhortation, or for that matter, made her feel any better. It's interesting to note that her son went on to get his Ph.D. at an Ivy League school, married a non-believer, and as far as I know, does not currently walk with the Lord.

Jesus said, *"You know that those who are regarded as rulers of the Gentiles lord it over them, and their high officials exercise authority over them. Not so with you. Instead, whoever wants to become great among you must be your servant, and whoever wants to be first must be slave of all."* The woman's son was very intelligent, and just because he wasn't valedictorian, it didn't hold him back from gaining scholarships, excelling at university, and getting his doctorate. The big question, however, is how is his spiritual life? Not very good. And he's not alone. Studies show that perhaps only one out of ten teenagers who grow up walking with the Lord, by the time they finish college, will still be faithful.

I have seen that statistic realized in my own ministry. A lot of our teens were strong in their faith in high school, but most are not walking with the Lord now. Why? Because in the final analysis, it was their parents' faith, not their own that kept them going to church. They never truly embraced the notion of obedience to God. It didn't supersede educational excellence, peer acceptance, or material accumulation. The unspoken lesson they were taught was that, if you want to be happy in life, then establish and maintain a great career, make a ton of money, and build up your social and recreational life. And if you have any time left over, give it to God. The Lord deserves more than our leftovers. It is more important to be obedient to God's calling than to excel in the world.

3. It is more important to point people to *Jesus* than to point people back to *ourselves*.

Elizabeth's story is only recorded in the first chapter of Luke. There is no other mention of her saga in any of the other gospels or in the entire New Testament. But even though we don't see her name, we see her personal imprint and influence through the legacy she left in her son John. Listen to his words:

- To the unbelievers asking who he was: "'*A prophet, Elijah?*' John replied, '*I am A VOICE OF ONE CRYING IN THE WILDERNESS, MAKE STRAIGHT THE WAY OF THE LORD.*'"

- To his own disciples who were complaining that more people were following Jesus than John, he said, "*He must increase; I must decrease.*"

- When Jesus, himself, came to John at the Jordan River asking to be baptized by him, he replied, "*I am not worthy to carry your sandals. You come to me to be baptized? I need to be baptized by you!*"[29]

---

[29] John 1:23, 3:30; Matthew 3:13-14 NIV

Where did John learn such humility? The answer is obvious – from his parents. John realized that it is more important to point people to Jesus than to himself. We all desire to raise our children to have this humble attitude, but we're afraid that the results of such humility might be a life of pain and suffering.

It reminds me of a pastor friend of mine who related story: a father came to him and said that he needed help in turning his boy around. "Pastor, take him under your wing, and make him a godly young man." My friend took on the task. A few months later, the father came back to him and said, "Pastor, you did *too good* of a job. My son wants to go into full-time ministry!" Be careful what you ask for! Being a pastor is a noble call, but the unspoken concern was that, if his son chose ministry as an occupation, he'd live in poverty like John the Baptist. But how do we define poor and by whose definition is rich?

> Where did John learn such humility? The answer is obvious – from his parents.

One day, a father of a very wealthy family took his son on a trip to the country with the firm purpose of showing his son how poor people can really be. They spent a couple of days and nights on the farm of, what would be considered, a very poor family.

On their return from their trip, the father asked his son, "How was the trip?"

"It was great," the son replied.

"Did you see how poor people can be?" the father asked.

"Oh, yeah," said the son.

"So what did you learn from the trip?" asked the father.

The son answered, "I saw that we have one dog and they had four.

"We have a pool that reaches to the middle of our garden and they have a creek that has no end.

"We have imported lanterns in our garden and they have the stars at night.

"Our patio reaches to the front yard and they have the whole horizon.

"We have a small piece of land to live on and they have fields that go beyond our sight.

"We buy our food, but they grow theirs.

"We have walls around our property to protect us; they have friends to protect them."

With this, the boy's father was speechless. Then his son added, "Thanks dad for showing me how poor we are."

The greatest thing our children can accomplish in life is not being the star of their little league team, or making valedictorian of their high school, or getting into an Ivy league university, or earning a six-figure salary, or having a mansion for a home. The greatest aim we can have our children accomplish is that, through our influence, they would desire to point people to Christ, that they would be like Jesus, that they would walk, talk, and live out their lives like the Lord.

> **The greatest thing we could see our children accomplish is that through our influence they would desire to point people to Christ**

That's the legacy of Elizabeth. She raised a second-fiddle son, who turned out just like mom, faithful in taking the focus off of himself and, instead, pointed people to Jesus.

Taking Time to Get Real

Heart-to-Heart

Ponder this question: What is the greatest sin? Maybe you came up with murder. Maybe it was adultery. Maybe you are super spiritual and believe that it is not believing in Jesus.

Those are all good answers, but the truth is that the greatest sin is pride. Pride caused the Lord's top angelic being, Satan, to think he could do a better job of being god than God. Pride caused a humble servant like David to look down from his rooftop and believe he had the right to take another man's wife. And pride, if we were honest, has caused us to stray away from God.

Take some time to meditate and pray. Ask the Lord where you have demonstrated pride, where you have put down others, have elevated yourself, and have made yourself out to be the god of your life.

Questions for Discussion

- If you have a sibling or siblings, or maybe cousins or good friends growing up, discuss how you were compared to them. How did it make you feel?

- What expectations were placed upon you by your parents? How has that affected you, in terms of your ambitions? How has it affected your desires for your own children?

- Assuming that you have been jealous of another at some time in your life, what caused that feeling? How, if ever, were you able to overcome it?

- What do you believe will be your greatest legacy? Why do you believe this to be true?

- Ponder this truth: It is more important to be number two in God's kingdom than number one in the world's eyes. In what ways have you placed a premium in being the best in the arenas of education, occupation, and athletics? Has this emphasis caused you to put your faith in a secondary role, and if so, how and why?

- Ask someone close to you to answer this question truthfully: When people think of my character and accomplishments…?
    a) I get the glory.
    b) My parents get the glory.
    c) my school gets the glory.
    d) my company/employer gets the glory.
    e) God gets the glory.
    How does their response make you feel?

Memory Verse: Mark 10:42-45

Jesus called them together and said, "You know that those who are regarded as rulers of the Gentiles lord it over them, and their high officials exercise authority over them. Not so with you. Instead, whoever wants to become great among you must be your servant, and whoever wants to be first must be slave of all. For even the Son of Man did not come to be served, but to serve, and to give his life as a ransom for many."

Heartwork

Take out two sheets of paper. On the first, write down the qualities mentioned in Galatians 5:19-21, the acts of the sinful nature: sexual immorality, impurity, debauchery, idolatry, witchcraft, hatred, discord, jealousy, fits of rage, selfish ambition, dissensions, factions, envy, drunkenness, and orgies. Write down specific instances where you have displayed such proud behavior.

On the other sheet of paper, title it "The Fruit of the Spirit" and list them from Galatians 5:22-23: love, joy, peace, patience, kindness, goodness, faithfulness, gentleness, and self-control. As on the first sheet of paper, write down specific instances where you have displayed such humble behavior.

Cain

Tempering My Temper
Genesis 4:1-14

As a young man, I had the unfortunate opportunity of managing my grandmother's property. As a Christ-follower, I always wanted to treat the tenants with respect and try to be as gracious with them, if at all possible. One gentleman got behind on his rent, and I tried to help him out. I allowed him to pay weekly and to do some handiwork in lieu of rent, but it just wasn't working out. Eventually, he got three months behind in rent and, to make matters worse, I found out that he was stealing electricity from the restaurant below by running an electrical line to his apartment. On several visits, I noticed garbage piled up in the apartment, and the water had been turned off. I reluctantly began the eviction proceedings.

To make a long story short: in court, he painted me to be a slumlord and threatened to take his case to a jury trial. My attorney strongly recommended that we settle out of court because, if my tenant should win the trial, it would be extremely costly. The judge dismissed the three months of rent, asked us to return his full deposit, and requested that I give my tenant an extra month to move out. What bothered me so much about this sordid situation is that I bent over backward for this guy when he was down and out, and he seemed really appreciative at the time; but in court, he lied through his teeth, making me out to be the bad guy. When I left the courtroom and saw him going down the stairs, he gave me this knowing smirk. I'll be honest – I was so angry at that moment, that if I could have gotten away with it, I would have hired a gang member to have him break his legs.

At this moment, you might be wondering, how could a pastor allow such a situation to get him so heated up? I could give you the excuse that I wasn't a pastor at the time, just a humble layperson in the church. But if you have pacifistic tendencies, you've probably lost a little respect for me. Or you may feel I'm perfectly justified. Not only would you cheer me on to seek justice, if you had the means, you'd seek out some individuals who could help me with my "request" (visions of scenes from the film *The Godfather* just came to mind).

Though we could be somewhat justified in our sense of injustice, manifesting our resentment to the point of physical violence suggests an anger problem. Maybe you would never imagine breaking someone's legs, but if you were honest, you'd have to admit that at some time you've harbored some pretty ugly thoughts toward others who've hurt you. You can look to the right and left in your church service, you'll see the quiet, silver-haired grandmother who never speaks above a whisper, the new mother who seems only focused on lavishing even more attention on her newborn, the soccer dad who has nothing but encouraging words for the students in his 3rd-grade Sunday School class – believe it or not, they've blown their stacks on many occasions, harboring ugly thoughts, and spewing harsh words.

We may never see it, but someone close to them has seen it, and it wasn't pretty.

All About Anger

In this chapter, we want to learn what anger is and how to deal with it. First, we have to differentiate between two types of anger. Feeling and displaying anger isn't necessarily a sin. There is a righteous anger. All we have to do is open one of the gospels and see that Jesus displayed a type of anger that was appropriate. In an incident recorded in Mark 3, Jesus compassionately healed a man with a withered hand. The religious leaders, however, were indignant because he healed the man on the Sabbath, which to them was a sin because you're not supposed to do work on the Sabbath. Look at Jesus' response to these gentlemen:

> "He looked around at them in <u>anger</u> and, deeply distressed at their stubborn hearts, said to the man, 'Stretch out your hand.' He stretched it out, and his hand was completely restored."[30]

In righteous anger, we note three attributes that Jesus displayed:

1. Rather than being indignant, the Lord manifested his anger by *grieving* over the religious leaders' hardness of heart.

---

[30] Mark 3:5-6 NIV

2. Jesus separated the individual from his/her poor *attitude* and *actions*.

3. His focus wasn't on being personally hurt, but rather, on God and his righteousness being *offended*.

In these three ways, we see that Jesus' anger was righteous. There's also an unrighteous anger. This is the type of anger that the Apostle James spoke of in his little letter:

> *"My dear brothers, take note of this: Everyone should be quick to listen, slow to speak and slow to become angry, for man's anger does not bring about the righteous life that God desires."*[31]

The Story of Cain

This type of unrighteous anger was manifested in a man named Cain. Let's recall his story which begins in Genesis 4:

> *"Adam lay with his wife Eve, and she became pregnant and gave birth to Cain. She said, 'With the help of the LORD I've brought forth a man.' Later she gave birth to his brother Abel. Now Abel kept flocks, and Cain worked the soil."*[32]

---

[31] James 1:19-20 NIV
[32] Genesis 4:1-2 NIV

We see that the first human parents were blessed with two boys. The older, Cain, was a farmer, a tiller of the soil. His younger brother Abel was a shepherd, a keeper of sheep. Both sons held honorable professions. Our text doesn't say anything about their early years, but boys being boys, I'm sure they had their share of fights. Can you hear them interacting? "Mom, Cain won't let me go with him to the field" "Dad, Abel keeps following me everywhere." "Quit looking at me." "Don't touch my food." Though we never want to see our children fight, we understand that daily squabbles are normal behavior. But when the boys were young adults, a more severe problem arose one day when they went to make an offering to the Lord:

> "In the course of time Cain brought some of the fruits of the soil as an offering to the LORD. But Abel brought fat portions from some of the firstborn of his flock. The LORD looked with favor on Abel and his offering, but on Cain and his offering he did not look with favor."[33]

As we move further on in Genesis 4, we learn about five facets of anger.

Five Characteristics That Mark the Unrighteously Angry Person

1. The root of unrighteous anger is the angry person, not others.

---

[33] Genesis 4:3-5a NIV

Our text says that both young men brought sacrifices to the Lord, and the Lord favored Abel's offering, but not Cain's. *"So Cain was very angry..."*[34]

You might be thinking, Cain had a right to be angry. He brought an offering just like his younger brother. Why didn't God accept it? Why did he show favoritism with Abel? First, we need to understand why God would have favored Abel's offering over Cain's. It wasn't because meat was more valuable than fruit. In the Old Testament, we see that God accepted both animal and grain sacrifices. But the one thing that God requires of any sacrifice from us is that it is always our best.

> **The one thing that God requires of any sacrifice from us is that it is always our best.**

If you read the text carefully, you see that Abel brought the first born, *the best*, the fattest lamb. It also says that Cain brought *some* of the fruits. From the text, we might deduce that Cain, with a lackadaisical attitude, meandered through his orchard, picking fruit with no special regard to the significance of their use. He ended up with a basket of bruised, scarred, and wormy apples, something we wouldn't give to our children, let alone offer to God. Abel, on the other hand, went to his flock and carefully and intentionally looked for the best of his animals: a lamb without blemish, perfect in every way.

It reminds me of the story of a woman who, in cleaning out her freezer, found a turkey that had been in storage for ten years. She called her butcher and asked if it was still eatable. "Yes, you can cook it, ma'am, but it probably won't

---

[34] Genesis 4:5b NIV

have much flavor," he said. She replied, "Oh, that's fine, I'll donate it to the church." What do you think: is she more like Cain or Abel? What about you, who are you more like?

In any case, Cain may have been blaming his brother or even God for his anger, but the root cause was his lax attitude toward worship of the Almighty. He gave God his leftovers, and God deserves our best. The root of Cain's unrighteous anger was himself.

2. Unrighteous anger is escalated by having a poor countenance.

> "...So Cain was very angry, and his face was downcast. Then the LORD said to Cain, 'Why are you angry? Why is your face downcast? If you do what is right, will you not be accepted? But if you do not do what is right, sin is crouching at your door; it desires to have you, but you must master it.'"[35]

You can't see it in English, but that word used for "downcast" literally means to have your face fall. It's a great word-picture for those who are angry – the furrowing of the brow, the clenched teeth, the eyes whose stare could melt steel. Have you ever thought about your countenance, the way your face presents your mindset? Some people seem to wear an eternal scowl, while others have crow's feet, due to a lot of smiling. The point is that many times an angry countenance can feed our feelings. It's hard to stay angry

---

[35] Genesis 4:5b-7 NIV

when you smile. Try it sometime. It's impossible. But it's easy to be angry with a frown.

God goes on to tell Cain that, when you allow your mind, body and face to feed upon your hatred, you open yourself up to sin. He says that sin is crouching at the door of your heart. The word-picture of sin is like a lion sitting in a cave, watching its prey walk by, waiting to pounce. God says that we should control ourselves, control our anger.

3. Repressed anger will eventually explode into rage.

> *"Now Cain said to his brother Abel, 'Let's go out to the field.' And while they were in the field, Cain attacked his brother Abel and killed him."*[36]

We don't know how much time had passed from the incident of the sacrifices, but Cain suggested the two brothers go back to work. I don't think it was Cain's intention to kill his brother. Perhaps what happened is that Cain was tending to his orchard and, looking over his shoulder, he saw his brother with a little lamb in his arms. Thoughts began to enter his head of what had transpired, and the resentment began to elevate. It grew in intensity until, finally, there was an explosion, and in that moment of unfettered rage, Cain the older murdered Abel the younger.

When I was in grade school, like a lot of boys, I loved firecrackers. One time, I found an empty rifle shell and I drilled a hole into the back of it. I placed a firecracker inside and pulled the fuse through the hole. I, then, put a lead split

---

[36] Genesis 4:8 NIV

shot used for fishing and crammed it into the hole. I, then, put the bullet in a vise grip in the garage, lit the firecracker, and put my fingers over my ears. Boom! The explosion was deafening, the fumes noxious, and the smoke made everything a haze. I looked at the cartridge and the split shot was gone. I looked across to the other side of the garage and there was the split shot, lodged deep in the sheet rock. Too cool! (Parents, not to scare you, but if you didn't know it already, these are the kinds of things your boys do. I could tell you about jumping off our house rooftop with an umbrella, but I'll save it for another lesson.)

What I experienced that fine day was a simple law of physics. Things under pressure, when a catalyst is introduced, will explode. Some people show their emotions all over their faces, but others hide them well. These types of people seem calm and always at ease, but all it takes is something to trigger them and boom! Explosion! We see this kind of reaction in the news all the time. The coworker or next door neighbor insists the murderer was a sweetheart, would never hurt anyone, was always pleasant, only to find out that he took an assault rifle and shot up his *former* place of employment.

Growing up as an Asian-American, I have been taught since childhood to hold in my emotions. The anger may not show visibly on my face, but the pain in my heart is still there. I like what John Powell said, "When I repress my emotions, my stomach keeps score." You can control your expressions, but you can't control the feelings. Eventually, the pressure builds and, like the firecracker lit by a spark, you explode.

> "When I repress my emotions, my stomach keeps score."

4. **A person with unrighteous anger refuses to take ownership for the problem.**

   "Then the LORD said to Cain, 'Where is your brother Abel?' 'I don't know,' he replied. 'Am I my brother's keeper?'"[37]

I always enjoy taking time to teach the children in our Awana[38] program. One time, I asked them if they had said anything mean to one another. Hands shot up immediately throughout the classroom. With some further probing, I found out that the one they usually got the angriest with was a younger sibling. Some of us feel like Cain. We watch a younger brother or sister or good friend stray. We've done everything we can to help them, but to no avail, and then we throw up our hands in exasperation and come to the conclusion, "Hey, I'm not his keeper." Unfortunately, Scripture says otherwise. We are our brother's and sister's keeper. We are accountable to them and for them. But like Cain, we try to escape accountability by putting the blame on others.

> **We are our brother's and sister's keeper. We are accountable to them and for them.**

---

[37] Genesis 4:9 NIV
[38] Awana stands for "Approved Workmen Are Not Ashamed," taken from 2 Timothy 2:15.

We do that by using the word "if." Cain certainly did: "*If* God didn't play favorites...*If* I was a shepherd...*If* Abel hadn't had that smirk on his face..." We get involved with a similar blame game: "*If* my parents weren't so protective...*If* my teacher wouldn't pick on me...*If* my boss didn't play me against my coworkers...*If* my husband would just do what I want." The problem with this kind of thinking is that conditions don't always go our way. We have to take ownership for our own problems.

5. A consistently angry person will always be avoided.

> "*The LORD said, 'What have you done? Listen! Your brother's blood cries out to me from the ground. Now you are under a curse and driven from the ground, which opened its mouth to receive your brother's blood from your hand. When you work the ground, it will no longer yield its crops for you. You will be a restless wanderer on the earth.' Cain said to the LORD, 'My punishment is more than I can bear. Today you are driving me from the land, and I will be hidden from your presence; I will be a restless wanderer on the earth, and whoever finds me will kill me.'*"[39]

Please note, in this whole dialogue between God and Cain that Cain never once admitted to the sin of murder. He never acknowledged that he was at fault for his brother's death or for being angry at God. The only one that an unrighteous, angry person thinks about is himself. We see

---
[39] Genesis 4:10-14 NIV

that readily with Cain. A person who is angry and won't let go of taking revenge is marked for life. From that day forward, Cain would live in fear of his safety because he wasn't willing to confess his sin.

You can see from Cain's response that he was bitter, pessimistic, and cynical, and who wants to be around these types of people? Proverbs 22:24-25 says, *"Do not make friends with a hot-tempered man, do not associate with one easily angered, or you may learn his ways and get yourself ensnared."* If you're constantly cantankerous, everyone will avoid you and, even more importantly, God can't work through you.

This is the problem that ensnares us when we give into unrighteous anger. Fortunately, Scripture never leaves us wallowing in sin, but always provides a solution on how to deal with our problems. We find that there are three positive steps that each of us can take toward controlling unrighteous anger:

Steps to Overcoming Unrighteous Anger

Step #1 – Repent: 1 John 1:9

> *"If we confess our sins, he* [Jesus] *is faithful and righteous and will forgive us our sins."*

Repentance is one of those spiritual words we bandy around, perhaps not fully understanding what we're talking about. But what repentance means is that you want to turn 180 degrees from the wrong direction, in which you were going. You have to admit that you've done wrong, and you have to resolve to own up to your unrighteous anger. When you repent, *truly repent*, and confess your sin to God. He can be depended on to forgive us and to cleanse us from every wrong.[40] This, of course, includes unrighteous anger. Please note that the primary focus of repentance is *upward* and is directed toward our relationship with *God*.

> The primary focus of repentance is *upward* and is directed toward our relationship with *God*.

Step #2 – Reconcile: Matthew 5:23-24

> *"So if you are standing before the altar in the Temple, offering a sacrifice to God, and suddenly remember that a friend has something against you, leave your sacrifice there beside the altar and go and apologize and be reconciled to him, and then come and offer your sacrifice to God."*[41]

Note that reconciliation is dealing with the fact that someone has something against you, not the other way around. Rather than harbor resentment toward the other, approach the relationship through reconciliation. Yes, it's humbling and maybe even humiliating.

Jim Andrews, a former professor at Western Seminary, once said that within every reconciliation, someone dies. Reconciling yourself to another is humbling because you die to yourself. But God honors humble people, not proud ones. In fact, your relationship with God is affected if you don't

---

[40] 1 John 1:9 TLB
[41] Matthew 18:23-24 TLB

> The primary focus of reconciliation is *outward* and is directed toward our relationship with *others*.

make the move toward reconciliation. God doesn't want your sacrifice or service if you're not willing to sacrifice and serve your brother or sister in Christ. The primary focus of reconciliation is *outward* and is directed toward our relationship with *others*.

Step #3 – Release: Matthew 18:23-35

In Matthew 18:23-35, the disciples ask Jesus how often should we forgive a brother who has sinned against us – seven times as prescribed by the Jewish law? Jesus says, *"No, seventy times seven."* Of course, he's not applying simple math, meaning we should forgive only 490 times, but rather, an *infinite* amount of times. The point is that the person who hurt you isn't perfect, but then neither are you. Paul tells us in Romans 5 to forgive others as Christ has forgiven us. Why should God forgive our sins when we won't forgive the sins of another?

> The primary focus of releasing our anger is *inward*, and is directed toward *me*.

You might be thinking to yourself, this person doesn't deserve to be forgiven for what they've done. Justice demands that they shouldn't be forgiven for what they did to me. That may be true, but forgiveness, the release of anger, is not a matter of *justice*, but rather, of *grace*. If you refuse to forgive and harbor resentment toward that person, guess who loses? Not them – they keep living on as if nothing happened. Who ends up losing is you because you'll allow your anger and resentment to eat away at your life. The primary focus of releasing our anger is *inward*, and is directed toward *me*.

A Personal Story...

My senior pastor was asked to leave our church in my third year of ministry at my present church. As the lone subordinate, I was now made, by default, the interim senior pastor. There was a gentleman (I use the term loosely), who had a difficult time with how the senior pastor was dismissed. An incident occurred with this man where the Chairman of the Deacon Board and his youngest son were physically threatened by him because he blamed the Chairman for our senior pastor's dismissal.

As the lone under-shepherd, I knew it was my duty to be the mediator in this situation. I wrote a letter to the gentleman, informing him that until we dialogued, he was not to be involved in any leadership roles at our church. This member took that letter around the congregation and highlighted a portion that seemed to imply that I was "kicking him out of the church." This caused many younger believers under the gentleman's ministry to become upset with me. Some were even crying about it. This man later called me on a Saturday evening, threatening to do something disruptive during the service. Since I had counseled him in a previous conflict, where he confided in me that he desired to go into his workplace and shoot his boss, you can understand that, during the next morning's worship service, I couldn't help but think that my life was potentially at risk. Praise God that nothing occurred.

For the next few years, I harbored a deep resentment toward this man. It didn't take much for me to bad-mouth him in front of others. You can imagine, then, after all I had been through with this man, that I was incensed when I explained the situation to a pastor friend and he told me that I need to forgive him and move on. I couldn't believe my ears! *Forgive him?!!* After all the anguish he had caused in our congregation? After verbally threatening me? After keeping our church from moving forward in its ministries for two whole years? There was no way I was going to ask forgiveness from him. If anything, I looked forward to the day he would come crawling back to me on his hands and knees begging to be forgiven.

That day never happened, but God did have his hand on both our lives. I don't recall the specific instance, but I remember the Holy Spirit speaking to my heart saying, "You must ask forgiveness for the anger and hatred you've harbored toward this man." I wrestled with the conviction, but in the end, at a church retreat, I pulled him aside and asked him to forgive me for my bitter thoughts toward him.

I'd like to tell you that he responded in kind by hugging me and, with tears in his eyes, asked me to forgive him. Again, like I said before, that day never happened. My contriteness didn't change his feelings toward me. To this day, as far as I know, he still hates my guts. That's okay, because God only asks me to make the first move toward reconciliation. It's up to God to move the other's heart. God did a supernatural work in my life. I no longer have that seething feeling of hatred and resentment inside of me. It was released the day I confessed my sin to my Lord and asked this brother to forgive me.

Maybe you'd admit right now that you have an uncontrolled, unrighteous anger burning inside of you. No one is able to see it; you're a great actor, but the truth is that you're not just hurting yourself, you're hurting your spouse, your parents, your children and friends, and you're destroying your Christian witness to the unchurched in your sphere of association. You're causing yourself unneeded anxiety and resentment, and most of all, you're crippling your relationship with your Heavenly Father. Let's not make the same mistake as Cain. Let's learn to control the anger. Repent, reconcile, release.

> **God only asks me to make the first move toward reconciliation. It's up to God to move the other's heart.**

Taking Time to Get Real

Heart-to-Heart

Let's face it, we're all busy people. In the midst of our busyness, rarely do we take the time to assess the condition of our hearts. Ask the Holy Spirit to reveal to you those individuals with which you have had a deep, long resentment. Look up some of these verses and see how they might apply to your life:

Proverbs 15:1
Proverbs 15:18
Proverbs 16:32
Proverbs 19:11
Matthew 5:21-22
Ephesians 4:26-28
Colossians 3:8-9

Questions for Discussion

- How do you manifest your anger? Are you verbally abusive, physically destructive, emotionally manipulative? Do you repress your feelings?

- Do you ever catch yourself using the "if" excuse for rationalizing your anger and resentment toward another? Think of several examples where you've used "if" as an excuse.

- Look at the steps to overcoming anger:
  o Repent (upward focus to God)
  o Reconcile (outward focus to other)
  o Release (inward focus to self)
  What step do you struggle with the most? Why is this so?

- *"Within every reconciliation a death must occur."* Sometimes I picture asking for forgiveness from another like handing them a dagger and giving them permission to stab me. What prevents you from allowing you to humbly apologize for your anger?

- Recall your deepest hurtful experience. What happened and what is the status of the relationship with the person or persons who hurt you?

- Have you cut off a previously good relationship with someone? Do you believe that God wants to restore that relationship once again? Will you take the necessary steps toward restoration? Pray about it and then take action.

Memory Verse: Ephesians 4:29-32

Do not let any unwholesome talk come out of your mouths, but only what is helpful for building others up according to their needs, that it may benefit those who listen. And do not grieve the Holy Spirit of God, with whom you were sealed for the day of redemption. Get rid of all bitterness, rage and anger, brawling and slander, along with every form of malice. Be kind and compassionate to one another, forgiving each other, just as in Christ God forgave you.

Heartwork

Write down on a sheet of paper the names of those individuals who have hurt you, angered you, or betrayed you.

After each name, take the time to write the events, attitudes, and situations which caused this pain to occur. Write down what you feel about this person, and what you expect this person to do to make the situation right.

Now the most difficult part…what can you do to make this situation right? Pray about it, and ask the Holy Spirit to give you the strength to carry through with your resolution this very week.

David

Look at It From God's Perspective
1 Samuel 16:7, 17:45

If you've never taken a trip to Yosemite National Park, then you've missed out on what many consider to be the most spectacular natural wonder in the lower 48 states. I remember one of the first times that I stood at a precipice called Glacier Point, which sits 3000 feet above the valley floor.

Maybe you've had the opportunity to view an Ansel Adams print from this same vantage point, but honestly, Adam's artwork, as wonderful as it is, pales in comparison to the real thing. The first landmark you notice is the magnificent Half-Dome. You can almost imagine God shaping this structure with the palm of His hand. In the distance are Vernal and Nevada falls, which become torrential during the spring runoff. El Capitan, a sheer granite cliff, challenges even the most expert climbers, while Bridal Veil Falls attracts the romantics. *Truly inspiring!*

Now fast forward a few years later to when I was a church intern working with our college group. Our fellowship had already gone ahead to begin our annual spring retreat. My mentor pastor, a few collegians, and I were driving up one night later because we just came from a wedding.

It was a great three-hour trip and we were having a grand old time of fellowship, amusing ourselves the whole way. Coming from a highly congested area like the San Francisco Bay Area, you rarely get to enjoy the pitch black darkness of a clear spring night. That joy, however, quickly turned to terror, when as we were driving along a mountain road, our pastor thought he would be funny by turning off the van headlights. We're driving 50 mph and we couldn't see the road in front of us! The high pitch of our concerted screams was deafening. A few seconds later, while laughing hysterically, he turned the headlights back on. *Truly frightening!*

I bring up these two incidents because I think it illustrates a good point: All of us experience the same things in life, but we can have differing reactions. Yosemite Valley is enjoyed by tens of thousands of people every year. Some will leave the mountains saying, "Ho hum," while others will respond with an exhilarated, "Ahhh!" The difference is a matter of perspective.

A Matter of Perspective

As Christians, we live our lives looking at people and situations from one of two perspectives. The first is from our own vantage point – because of a lack of trust or faith, we look at difficult people and life's unexpected problems with fear and trepidation. It's as if we're driving in the dark without headlights. The alternative perspective is to see others and life not from our vantage point, but rather, from

God's viewpoint. That's difficult to do because, when dealing with people or decisions, most of the time, we choose the most familiar path. But Scripture tells us that the old nature is done away with. We have been transformed from the inside out and are new creatures in Christ (1 Corinthians 5:17). God is calling us to view life not from down below, but rather, from up above – the Lord wants us to see things from His *perspective*.

> God is calling us to view life not from down below, but rather, from up above

Perspective Defined

Perspective is defined as the capacity to view things from a different angle. It is a compound word composed of *per*, "through," and *specere*, "to look." How we think, form our attitudes, react emotionally, and propose certain actions come from our accumulated experiences; that is, how we've looked through our life's situations. Each of us has developed his/her own unique, personal perspective. When it is in line with God, it leads to a contented, fulfilled life. When it is not, we make mistakes, we prejudge, we sin.

Of course, this isn't how God wants it to be. As Christ-followers, we should be going through a continual spiritual growing process, shedding off the old ways of thinking and taking on the mindset of the Lord. This is a lesson that we learn from the life of David. The two events that we want to look at are found in 1 Samuel, and from them, we get a profound lesson on how to view life from God's perspective instead of our own.

In 1 Samuel 16:7, we have a timely verse that proclaims this very truth:

> *"But the Lord said to Samuel, 'Do not consider his appearance or his height, for I have rejected him. The Lord does not look at the things man looks at. Man looks at the outward appearance, but the Lord looks at the heart."*

My Elementary School Years...

Take a look at this photograph from my seventh grade junior high class:

SEVENTH GRADE HONOR ROLL

I'm the one in front on the right end (see the white arrow). Beyond the fact that I was cute as the dickens, you might also notice that I was the shortest kid in school, shorter even than Joan G. standing at the opposite corner, who was the next shortest kid in school. It was always that way for me because I grew up with chronic asthma and had been placed on some pretty powerful medications. My mother would take me to the clinic night after night, and the attending physicians would give me the usual shots of epinephrine and susphrine. My wheezing was controlled, but then my heart would be racing at 180 beats per minute.

My asthma was so severe that my parents sent me to the Stanford Children's Convalescent Home in Palo Alto, CA, for what would turn out to be six months...twice! I went for six months when I was four, and for six months when I was eight. I remember when I was twelve that I was terrified that I might have to go back for another six months.

At Stanford, the medical staff could attend to my poor health 24 hours a day. For the duration of my elementary years, I avoided playground activities and sports with the other children. Instead, I would go home at lunchtime and get on my own personal nebulizer. Maybe it was because I had to endure all these personal trials that my elementary school picked me as the "Most Inspirational Player" three years in a row. To be honest, I never thought of this award as a true honor because I knew they always gave this kind of prize to the pathetic athletes. Most of my school days were spent indoors. While the other kids played ball during recess, I was in the library. Get out the tissue... sniff, sniff.

My Junior High School Years...

Things didn't get much better for me in junior high. At thirteen years old, I was the kid others wanted to stuff in the garbage can for laughs. As in grade school, I spent my free time in the library, but I was forced to take PE like all the other kids. During my first trimester, all the boys had to take wrestling, the perfect sport for a squirt like me. My apprehension turned into terror when Coach Hoff barked out, "Quan, get out there!" Here I was, this little 7th grader, and he matched me up with George, a shorter, but stocky 8th grader. In the lingo of the time, he was what you'd call a "burnout." He and his buddies hung out under the bleachers smoking and carrying on. You could see by his smirk that George didn't think much of me as an opponent. Maybe he knew me as the kid who always hung out at the library. So here was the match of the day – geek versus freak! I think the odds were definitely in his favor.

So there I was on all fours, seventy-five lbs. of sinewy muscle, with this hoodlum's arm around my waist. I would have much preferred to be playing chess, but life dealt these kinds of situations. Ready, set, go! As you can imagine, it was over quickly, and it was quite humiliating…for George, that is. I pinned him with his legs dangling in mid-air in about ten seconds.

As this incident occurred over three decades ago, and I've been able to recall it quite vividly, you can imagine that this was a highlight for my life. But that's not my point. The point of this whole story is, if you had to make a choice back then on who would have won that wrestling match that fine spring afternoon in 1972, you would have picked George…and you would have been wrong. And so it goes with David.

God's Perspective on People: It Begins with Saul

We need to backtrack a little bit and get a picture of what was going on with Israel at the time. Israel was a theocracy. It was founded as a nation on the premise that God, not a king, would rule His people. But the people looked at the nations around them and decided that like them, they, too, wanted their own king. The Lord was gracious and chose Saul, a Benjamite, to rule over Israel. From a human perspective, he was a great choice – the Bible describes him as a head taller than any other man around, handsome, and a mighty man of valor.

To be fair, we have to give Saul credit for starting off his monarchy on the right track. At the beginning of his reign, he mustered up 300,000 troops and destroyed the Ammonites. He then went on to defeat the Philistines. He then led God's army in victory over Moab, Ammon, Edom, the kings of Zobah, Philistia again, and the Amalekites (1 Samuel 14:47-48). As a military leader, from a human perspective, Saul was a great choice to be king. He defeated every foe who crossed his path; so to his people, he was a hero.

The problem with Saul was not his very visible accomplishments, but rather, his invisible lack of character. It first manifests itself as *impatience*, when he decided to take matters into his own hands. He knew he was supposed to wait seven days for the prophet Samuel to oversee the burnt and peace offerings before going to war with the Philistines. When Samuel didn't show up on time, Saul went about overseeing the offerings himself, a no-no at that time because only the priest was to give the offering. His character issue surfaced again in *recklessness*, when he placed a curse on any man who would eat food before evening until he avenged himself against the Philistines. Unfortunately, his son Jonathan didn't hear of the curse and took some honey that day (1

> The problem with Saul was not his very visible accomplishments, but rather, his invisible lack of character.

Samuel 14:24-30). Now Saul would be forced under oath to kill his own son.

Saul's third and greatest blunder came when Samuel prophesied that he was to strike Amalek the king and destroy every living thing in his realm. The command was direct and straightforward:

> "Now go, attack the Amalekites and totally destroy everything that belongs to them. Do not spare them; put to death men and women, children and infants, cattle and sheep, camels and donkeys."[42]

Any lower elementary grade-school child can understand this command – see Amalek, see his people, see their animals. Kill them all. Wipe 'em all out! We'll see that Saul had a more nuanced way of looking at life. Perhaps he pondered, "Does *destroy* really mean put everything to death? I mean, what good does it do to kill off all the animals? They can be used for good. Why waste them on the altar?" This seemed to be King Saul's intention. Yes, he defeated the Amalekites, but he didn't follow through with the Lord's complete command:

> "Then Saul attacked the Amalekites all the way from Havilah to Shur, to the east of Egypt. He took Agag king of the Amalekites alive, and all his people he totally destroyed with the sword. But Saul and the army spared Agag and the best of the sheep and cattle, the fat calves and lambs – everything that was good. These they were unwilling to

---

[42] 1 Samuel 15:3 NIV

destroy completely, but everything that was despised and weak they totally destroyed."[43]

King Saul, along with the people, was rejoicing over the defeat of their enemy. But the prophet Samuel came along and spoiled the victory parade. Saul bragged to the prophet about carrying out the Lord's command, and Samuel countered by saying, *"What then is this bleating of the sheep in my ear, and the lowing of the oxen that I hear?"* The king's lame excuse was that the people spared the best so that they might be sacrificed to the Lord. The prophet stopped him in mid-sentence...

"Does the LORD delight in burnt offerings and sacrifices as much as in obeying the voice of the LORD?

To obey is better than sacrifice, and to heed is better than the fat of rams.

For rebellion is like the sin of divination, and arrogance like the evil of idolatry.

Because you have rejected the word of the LORD, he has rejected you as king."[44]

King Saul was mighty in military strength and valor, but he was weak in godly character and virtue. Before Samuel had time to get depressed over the matter, the Lord consoled the prophet and told him that he'd chosen another to take Saul's place. *"Go to Jesse, the Bethlehemite, for I desire to make*

---

[43] 1 Samuel 15:7-9 NIV
[44] 1 Samuel 15:22-23 NIV

one of his sons to be the next king." Samuel made the trek to Bethlehem to look for God's anointed sovereign.

The Choosing of a King

The first son that greets Samuel is Jesse's eldest, Eliab. Like Saul, he, too, is strong, tall, and handsome. He is also a military commander serving under King Saul. What better choice to be the next king than Eliab? Great from a human perspective, but not from God's, and he tells Samuel as much:

> *"Do not consider his appearance or his height, for I have rejected him. The LORD does not look at the things man looks at. Man looks at the outward appearance, but the LORD looks at the heart."*[45]

Of all the people who should have figured out that the Lord was not interested in what you looked like on the outside, but who you were inside, you'd think Samuel would have gotten it. The prophet had just witnessed the Lord dethrone Saul for his lack of character and disobedience. And now days later, he looked upon this kingly prospect from a human perspective, the perfect choice in man's eyes, but not from God's vantage point. Samuel didn't get it.

Okay, it's not Eliab...bring on the next! In walked Abinadab, who was not as impressive as Eliab, but was a pretty good choice...from a human perspective...but again, not

---
[45] 1 Samuel 16:7 NIV

according to God. Next! Out of door #3 walked Shammah. Nope, the Lord hadn't chosen him either…nor sons number four through number seven. Exasperated, Samuel called out to the dad, "Jesse, this can't be it. You must have some other sons. The Lord wouldn't steer me wrong on this one."

"Well, I do have one more son. His name is David, a good looking lad, but he's just a boy. He's out tending our sheep in the field."

David was probably no more than twelve at the time, a spunky junior-higher. But this kid was to eventually be not only Israel's greatest king, but also declared by God to be a man after his own heart.

Hindsight is always 20/20 isn't it? And it would be so easy to put down Samuel for not seeing that David was God's anointed servant. But let's be honest, we'd have to admit that, given the same choice, we would have made the same assumptions as him. If you had to choose the next king of Israel, would you pick a thirty-something year old, experienced military leader who was tall, strong, and handsome? Or would you choose a gangly, good-looking twelve-year-old boy who took care of sheep? Like Samuel, we evaluate people from a human perspective, not necessarily from God's perspective.

Personal Eye Exam #1

Think about yourself in these kinds of situations. Ponder who you thought would be better suited to be a children's Sunday School teacher, or who, after all these years, would be the friend who stuck by you during the worst of times, or the best person to minister with on your mission trip. Did it surprise you that the person you thought would be the best turned out to be the most challenging, while the one you thought would crash and burn was the most successful? It shouldn't surprise us. The Lord says that external measurements are not to be trusted; you have to look inside at the heart and character of a person. And the Bible is replete with examples of God doing just that.

Rahab was a pagan prostitute who most people avoided when they crossed her path on Main Street, and yet her name is recorded in Hebrews 11, the so-called "hall of faith," because she trusted the Lord and hid the Israelite spies.[46] Gideon was a timid, cowardly man who hid in a wine vat to avoid his enemies, but he was tested by God and became an incredibly effective judge who saved his people from the marauding Midianites.[47]

Finally, look at the men the Lord Jesus picked to be his initial followers; they weren't religious teachers, political leaders, or high profile businessmen. Rather than movers and shakers, he chose a rough hodgepodge of blue-collared nobodies, who just happened to teachable and, thus, wholly dedicated to God.

How about you? When someone new comes into your fellowship or cell group, are you apt to assess their fit into your ministry before you even say one word to them? Or as a single, what are the qualities that draw you to a potential mate; are they primarily external or internal, material or spiritual? As a student, who are you planning to choose to be in your study group; is it based on the person's potential GPA or on his/her ability to get along and work as a team?

---

[46] Hebrews 11:31 NIV
[47] Judges 8:28 NIV

> It's easy to take the path of least difficulty, to choose the familiar, the stronger, the wealthier, the more popular, the most powerful or the best looking. But God shows us a different way.

It's easy to take the path of least difficulty, to choose the familiar, the stronger, the wealthier, the more popular, the most powerful or the best looking. But God shows us a different way. To really manifest his power, we need to be able to see with spiritual eyes beyond what is obvious and to look at the heart.

God's Perspective on Problems: It Ends with Goliath

There's a second area where I think we have problems seeing things from God's perspective. Not only do we evaluate *people* from an earthly perspective, but we also do the same with our *problems*. We see this played out in a second incident that occurred in the life of David.

It is a few years later, and even though we know David will eventually be king, at this time Saul was still the sovereign of Israel. The Israelites were warring with the Philistines. Lined up for battle over a valley outside of Jerusalem, God's people were squared off against God's enemies. In the enemy's corner, their hero, a giant named Goliath called out a challenge to the Israelites:

> *"Do you need a whole army to settle this? I will represent the Philistines, and you choose someone to represent you, and we will settle this in single combat! If your man is able to kill me, then we will be your slaves. But if I kill him,*

then you must be our slaves! I defy the armies of Israel! Send me a man who will fight with me!"[48]

Put into the vernacular, Goliath was trying to make it easy for everyone. "Forget a bloody war that leaves thousands of dead on the battlefield. Let's make this *mano y mano* between me and your strongest warrior. Winner take all!"

If this battle were fought today, we might send a giant of a man like Shaquille O'Neal. But the NBA center would have stood a good two feet shorter and 225 lbs. lighter than Goliath. The Bible says that Goliath wore 200 lbs. of armor and carried a javelin with a shaft that was several inches thick. The tip weighed 25 lbs.!

As you might imagine, the men of Israel cowered in fear before this giant warrior. At about this time, David came on the scene to deliver food for his brothers in the battle field. He overheard this blowhard's taunts, and he responded in a manner that would suggest not only youthful exuberance, but also immaturity..."*Who is this heathen Philistine, anyway, that he is allowed to defy the armies of the living God?"*[49]

David's bravado was duly noted by the Israelite officers and was reported back to Saul. So the king sent for him. Before Saul, David once again stated his desire to battle Goliath. Seeing no other means of victory, the king reluctantly offered his own armor to the boy, but he's so slight, it just slipped right off of him! It didn't matter anyway, because David knew he didn't need armor for protection against the Philistine; he had the God of the Universe on his

---

[48] 1 Samuel 17:8-10 TLB
[49] 1 Samuel 17:26 TLB

side. He then headed out onto the battlefield with merely a sling and five stones.

Goliath eyed the lad coming forward to fight him and was taken aback. In disgust, he called out, *"Am I a dog, that you come at me with sticks?"* He then cursed David by his gods. *"Come here, and I'll give your flesh to the birds of the air and the beasts of the field!"*[50]

These words were meaningless to David. He set the giant straight on the reality of the situation:

> *"You come against me with sword and spear and javelin, but I come against you in the name of the Lord Almighty, the God of the armies of Israel, whom you have defied."*[51]

Personal Eye Exam #2

We all know how this showdown eventually ends because it is one of the most famous battles ever fought. (For those of you who don't know the outcome...David wins.) But here's the million dollar question: If you were asked to place a bet (of course you don't gamble) on who would win this match, who would you have picked? Conventional wisdom says that to overcome a problem, you need strength, intellect, wealth, and/or authority. This same reasoning leads us to believe that to ensure getting a decent job, I *must* have a good education from a top university. I *need* meaningful experiences to keep that job and to be promoted. The promotion *will* grant me authority to get things done. The

---

[50] 1 Samuel 17:43-44 NIV
[51] 1 Samuel 17:45 NIV

higher position *means* more money which allows me to buy my way out of my problems. You need intellect, strength, wealth, and authority to overcome problems.

General Norman Schwarzkopf, commander of the Allied Forces against Iraq in early 1991, wrote a book, *It Doesn't Take a Hero,* where he details what happened in Desert Storm. In his book, he mentions that in any ideal military situation, to ensure victory over your enemy, you must outnumber them 2 to 1. Military success comes through dominance.

The same principle holds true in the sports world. Pick any successful professional franchise and behind it will be an owner who is willing to spend the money to win, a brilliant coach who not only understands the game, but knows how to motivate his players, a gifted superstar or two, and a cohesive powerful team. We love to think that any team can win a championship, but the reality is that the Jamaican bobsled teams never win gold.

This is how the world works. The wealthy fat cats, the entrenched lobbyists, the connected powerbrokers, and Hollywood celebrities are the ones who make things happen. That's why investors listen to every word that comes out of the mouth of Warren Buffett. And the U.S. Senate will actually listen to the testimonies of celebrities like rock icon David Crosby on Indian affairs, and Hollywood star Sean Penn on Iraq, and TV star Michael J. Fox on Parkinson's disease.

But God has shown us through the story of David that there is a different way. We can overcome problems by having a different perspective. As overwhelming as your difficulties seem to be, God's power to provide and comfort is greater. David looked at a nine-foot tall, 550 lb. problem and saw an all knowing, all powerful, all loving solution.

You might be thinking to yourself, "This is a Bible story. My situation isn't like this. It might have worked in the time of the Ancients, but this is the 21st century." Situations are a little more complicated today. None of my problems take the form of a giant who wants to shish kabob me with his spear for sadistic entertainment. But my problems are just as serious. Bad relationships, health problems, stress in school, un-reliable car, difficult siblings, boring life, death of a loved one – all of these are problems that, at the very least, irritate me and, at the most, cause me to lose heart, to want to give up.

> As overwhelming as your difficulties seem to be, God's power to provide and comfort is greater.

Dr. Thomas Holmes at the University of Washington completed a study on stress. He co-developed the Social Readjustment Rating Scale which measured stress in terms of life changing units. He identified 43 specific stress-inducing events: death of a spouse – 100 units, divorce – 73 units, pregnancy – 40 units, remodeling a home – 25 units, and even Christmas - 12 units (Christmas was rated higher for those families with young children). His conclusion is that if you have over 300 units in a twelve-month period, you will suffer physically and/or emotionally.[52]

The truth is that, if we lived according to the principles of this world, we'd all eventually end up as basket cases. But we are not of this world, and Scripture confirms and reaf-

---

[52] Thomas Holmes, *Life Change, Life Events and Illness*, 1989.

firms our standing in Christ. Meditate upon these verses of promise:

> *"All things work together for good, to those who love God, to those called according to his purpose..."*
>
> *"If He be for us, who can be against us?"*
>
> *"I can do all things through him who strengthens me."*
>
> *"Be anxious for nothing, but in everything by prayer and petition let your requests be made known to God, and the peace of God which surpasses all comprehension will guard your heart and mind in Christ Jesus..."*
>
> *"Therefore I tell you, do not worry about your life, what you will eat or drink; or about your body, what you will wear. Is not life more important than food, and the body more important than clothes?...For the pagans run after all these things, and your heavenly Father knows that you need them. But seek first his kingdom and his righteousness, and all these things will be given to you as well."*[53]

A Personal Lesson on Wrong Perspective

When I first came to Greater Phoenix Chinese Christian Church in Chandler, AZ, in 1993, our congregation was small enough so that we could do some unusual things. One summer, we decided to forego Sunday School and, instead, went to visit various churches in the area to see how others worshipped.

---

[53] Romans 8:28, 8:31; Philippians 4:6-7, 4:13; Matthew 6:25, 32-33 NIV

On one occasion, we visited one of the largest African-American churches in Phoenix. The adults carpooled and helped bring our youth to an area of town that we, in suburban Chandler, would not normally visit.

We stayed only for about an hour as their service was longer than ours. We enjoyed the lively music and uplifting preaching, but I was getting a little nervous bringing my congregation to this part of town. As we left, I noticed a young African-American man in a new sports car, sun glasses shading his eyes – he was watching our members as they left the sanctuary. There I was standing in the middle of a parking lot in the worst part of town and we're being scoped out by a drug dealer! As I said my prayers to myself, I quickly herded our children into the minivans and we made our way out of the "ghetto" and back into the safe suburbs, where there was no graffiti, no drugs, and no gang members!

That week, I got a call from one of my members, who was an escort on that trip. He said excitedly, "Did you see the guy in the parking lot in the Mercedes convertible?" Before I could get a word in, he continued, "That was _____!" The name was recognizable immediately to me. He played forward for the Arizona State University basketball team and was recruited by the Phoenix Suns. He was also known to be a devout Christian.

If there was ever a time that I wished I saw a person and a situation from God's perspective instead of mine, it was then. My prejudice, which I'm embarrassed to admit, caused me to make a very wrong judgment. It was a great lesson for me, and one that I will never forget.

Gaining God's Perspective

What difficult person or insurmountable problem are you facing today? From a human perspective, you may have a wrong understanding of the situation, or you might believe that a solution seems impossible. But if we were to see our situation from God's perspective, we might understand that he has given us his Spirit and his power to overcome. Don't lose heart. God hasn't given up on you; he's just trying to help you know that he has a different take on your life. Let's resolve to view life from a different perspective, God's perspective.

1. See people as God sees them.
Overcome the desire for human prejudgment and utilize God's wisdom and word in evaluating and interacting with people.

2. See problems as God sees them.
They are not meant to be occasions to harass you, but as opportunities to strengthen you and to allow you to trust God to pull you through.

Taking Time to Get Real

Heart-to-Heart

We've been talking about seeing people and life's difficulties from God's perspective rather than our own. This, of course, is easier said than done. We naturally are comfortable with our viewpoint because it is what we are most familiar with. Therefore, it's almost impossible to gain God's perspective unless we get outside ourselves.

In ascertaining what wrong thinking or prejudices we're harboring, a good outside source is Scripture. Another way to gain a different perspective is through meditative prayer. One other means would be to consult with a person whom you trust, who will be honest and objective with you about your attitudes. Take time this week to shake yourself up.

Questions for Discussion

- Do you remember a time when you were prejudged? What happened in that specific incident and how did you feel?

- Recall a particular incident/trial/problem that seemed impossible to overcome, and then God came through for you. Why did it seem so impossible at the time, and how has that victory helped you to cope with the present ordeal that you're dealing with from God's perspective?

- Who do you turn to first when dealing with difficult problems? Be honest! Put the following list in ascending order: parents, siblings, friends, teachers, pastors, superiors, TV celebrities, online sources, God, other.

- Do you find that you turn to God only in specific types of instances? What are those instances and why only them and not all things?

- Have you cut off a previously good relationship with someone? Do you believe that God wants to restore that relationship once again? Will you take the necessary steps toward restoration? Pray about it and then take action.

Memory Verse: 1 Samuel 6:7, Philippians 4:6-7

Do not consider his appearance or his height, for I have rejected him. The LORD does not look at the things man looks at. Man looks at the outward appearance, but the LORD looks at the heart.

Be anxious for nothing, but in everything by prayer and petition let your requests be made known to God, and the peace of God which surpasses all comprehension will guard your heart and mind in Christ Jesus...

Heartwork

Being prejudiced does not necessarily have to do with racism. Prejudging happens any time we make assumptions about an individual or group of individuals without knowing the facts. In the concluding story, I made a huge prejudgment about an individual.

Take some time to write down the name of individuals, or groups of individuals (it might be a particular race, culture, fellowship group, church, denomination, even neighborhood or school), in which you've shown prejudgment.

Contemplate how this wrong perspective caused you to miss opportunities to minister to, befriend, or serve with them in the name of the Lord.

Jephthah

Be Careful What You Promise God
Judges 11:29-40

Early on in my ministry, I was very uncomfortable being around young children. But I had an excuse – I was single and forty years old. Except for a few times with my nieces, I never really had to associate with kids. And those children that I was forced to be around at church, namely the 5th and 6th grade boys, I found to be obnoxious, insensitive, and rough (come to think of it, they're a lot like me).

But something happened in my life that changed my animosity towards children…I had children of my own and, since then, I love interacting with and teaching kids. One Friday evening, I was sharing with the kids in our Awana program about *stewardship*, the fact that everything we supposedly own, in actuality, belongs to God; that being so, we need to be smart in how we use our resources. I talked about the *tithe*; that as believers, we should give at least 10% of our income to God and the Lord graciously allows us to keep 90% for ourselves.

One young boy shouted out, "When I get the money, I'll give God 90% and keep 10% for myself." I stared at him and thought, *a teaching moment*. I fixed my eyes on his and said, "What did you say?" He was a little more sheepish and mumbled the same words. I pointed at him in an almost accusatory fashion, "Be careful what you promise God. When you make an oath, you must keep it...or else!" I think it was the "or else" part that almost made him cry. (I said I love to be around kids, I didn't say they love to be around me.)

> **If you make a vow to God, you'd better be sure you take it serious.**

Promising the World...

Making a young boy bawl like a little baby was not my intent, but I wanted him and the other children to understand that, if you make a vow to God, you'd better be sure you take it seriously. This also reminds me of a film that came out a while ago that most of you have never seen or heard. It was entitled *The End*, with Burt Reynolds and Dom Deluise. It was a slapstick, dark comedy about a man who found that he hadn't much longer to live and how he kept bungling his attempts at suicide. Toward the end of the movie, he took the extreme measure of throwing himself out of a boat into the middle of the ocean. As he was about to drown, he reassessed his intent to die and decided he wanted to live. Far away from shore, his vows were lofty, outrageous. But as he got closer to shore, they became more mundane, to the point that, as he made it to shore, his promises to God were pretty much meaningless.

This film gives us a glimpse of how we sometimes act when we're in trouble. We'll promise God anything and everything if he'll get us out of a jam. The farce is not *if*, but *when* God is faithful and overcomes, we're left with a vow we never expected to keep. That's what we have with our next hero, a biblical judge by the name of Jephthah.

An Introduction to Jephthah

You might not know him like the other more famous judges, Gideon and Samson, because his pedigree was not so special. Samson was anointed before birth to greatness and raised by godly parents. Jephthah had no special announcement at his birth, and his mother was a prostitute. Even though his father was a nobleman, having a streetwalker for a mom totally undermined his stand in the family. His stepbrothers, children of his father's one and only "true" wife, had no regard for him.

So without the protection of his mother's family, he roamed the countryside and created a band of mercenaries. These fellow misfits took to his leadership and, soon enough, they became an incredible fighting force. Because he established himself as such a skilled fighter and commander, his people, the Gileadites, changed their mind and wanted him to be their commander. This position was especially important because it involved both military and political authority. They needed him especially now because the Ammonites wanted to destroy them. When he got in their face about their change of attitude toward him, they reassured their desire to have him lead them. They coroneted him and now he was in command.

We pick up the story of his strategy to fight the Ammonites in Judges 11:29-31:

> *"Then the Spirit of the LORD came upon Jephthah. He crossed Gilead and Manasseh, passed through Mizpah of Gilead, and from there he advanced against the Ammonites. And Jephthah made a vow to the LORD: 'If you give the Ammonites into my hands, whatever comes out of the door of my house to meet me when I return in triumph from the Ammonites will be the LORD's, and I will sacrifice it as a burnt offering.'"*

Jephthah was now the leader. Jephthah was expected to bring them victory over their enemies. Jephthah was also a man who believed in the goodness of Yahweh, and he knew that victory would only come through the provision and graciousness of God. And so, he made God a promise: "Lord, if you bring us victory, I'll sacrifice whatever comes out of my house."

A Rash Promise...

But what kind of sacrifice was he expecting? Yes, he said, "Whatever," but from the Hebrew that could also mean "whoever." Yes, animals in that time lived in homes. But don't expect Fido to come out because dogs weren't kept in homes at that time. In fact, most likely, Jephthah probably wasn't speaking of an animal because the sacrifice of an animal would not be worthy of the victory in such a great battle. We would have to deduce that Jephthah anticipated a human sacrifice. This would not be out of line with practices from the pagan nations in the Middle East at that time. Idomenus, king of Crete, is reported in classical literature to have vowed to sacrifice his son if his god would save him from the storms that threatened his return from sacking Troy. He made it back safely and he killed his son. Israel's surrounding neighbors worshipped Chemosh, the god of the Moabites, and the Bible records many instances of the sacrifice of children to this pagan god.

Please also note that Yahweh, the God of the Jews, never asked Jephthah to make this kind of vow, but somehow like many of us today, we expect God only to do great things if we make a big sacrifice. It's got to cost us or it's not going to be accepted.

Recall the story of Naaman (2 Kings 5), the Syrian general who had leprosy. He was sent by his king to be healed by the prophet Elisha. Elisha told him to wash in the Jordan seven times and he would be cured of his disease. Naaman's response was angry as he reasoned, "Aren't the rivers of Damascus much greater?" However, in the end, the general humbled himself and did as Elisha commanded and was healed. Naaman found victory, but think of the mentality he had in order to be healed. To be cured of this dreaded and deadly skin disease, he believed it called for extraordinary means. Elisha showed it wasn't the importance of the *sacrifice*, but rather, the intensity of the *faith* that mattered.

> **Elisha shows it wasn't the importance of the *sacrifice*, but rather, the intensity of the *faith* that mattered.**

Now getting back to our story, Jephthah fought the Ammonites. The results are found in verses 32 – 33:

> *"Then Jephthah went over to fight the Ammonites, and the LORD gave them into his hands. He devastated twenty*

towns from Aroer to the vicinity of Minnith, as far as Abel Keramim. Thus Israel subdued Ammon."

Against all odds, the Israelites were victorious. What an incredible success. They earned a ticker-tape parade and victory march when they got home. And that's what they got...but the celebration came with a price. Verses 34 – 35 state:

> *"When Jephthah returned to his home in Mizpah, who should come out to meet him but his daughter, dancing to the sound of tambourines! She was an only child. Except for her he had neither son nor daughter. When he saw her, he tore his clothes and cried, 'Oh! My daughter! You have made me miserable and wretched, because I have made a vow to the LORD that I cannot break.'"*

Look at how the writer of Judges sets up the story. Coming home victorious, who should Jephthah meet dancing and celebrating along with the women of the town, but his daughter, his *only* child. For further emphasis, the author added that he had "neither son nor daughter." Glorious triumph quickly turned to agonizing defeat for Jephthah. Carrying through with his vow would mean the end of his family line. It's interesting that he put the blame for his dilemma on his unsuspecting daughter. "Oh! My daughter! <u>You</u> have made me miserable and wretched..."

But note his daughter's response in verses 36 – 37...

> *"'My father,' she replied, 'you have given your word to the LORD. Do to me just as you promised, now that the*

LORD has avenged you of your enemies, the Ammonites. But grant me this one request,' she said. 'Give me two months to roam the hills and weep with my friends, because I will never marry.'"

As you read her brave words, remembrances of a past son come to mind. Isaac, the promised son of Abraham, willingly yielded himself to be sacrificed because it was the will of God. On the surface, the two children's situations seem similar, but there's a marked difference. The difference between the two is that God asked for the sacrifice of Isaac, whereas Jephthah was the instigator of his own quandary. The daughter took note of her agonizing father, and she understood the implications not only for him, but also for herself. But she didn't ask him to break his vow. For her, if victory over Ammon meant her death, she faced it willingly. It was worth it. To quote a line from the early Star Trek films, "The needs of the many outweighed the needs of the one."

A Disturbing Fulfillment

In spite of her bereavement, this daughter asked for one thing. It was the ultimate goal of every Hebrew woman to be married and bear children. In fulfilling her father's vow, she would not be able to do either. She asked for two months to weep with her friends over her perpetual virginity and absence of children. Verses 38 – 40:

"'You may go,' he said. And he let her go for two months. She and the girls went into the hills and wept because she would never marry. After the two months, she returned to her father and he did to her as he had vowed. And she was a virgin. From this comes the Israelite custom that each year the young women of Israel go out for four days to commemorate the daughter of Jephthah the Gileadite."

There's an incident that I recall which was so heinous at the time – a woman who suffered from post-partum depression cut off the arms of her one year old and waited for the police to arrest her. The child later died in the hospital. Since I had a two-year-old daughter at that time, this story was especially horrifying and tragic for me. I remembered thinking to myself, how could anyone do something so monstrous to her own child?

That's why when we read in the Bible about an incident like Jephthah and his daughter, it's just as disturbing. Many theologians believe that Jephthah didn't really kill his daughter. Instead, he dedicated her to the city temple to carry out the rest of her life for sanctuary service, remaining a virgin, never to marry nor have children.

This may be wishful thinking because there are four problems with this theory:

1. In Near East cultures at that time, those women dedicated to the temple would have been the exact opposite, that is not temple virgins, but rather, temple prostitutes.

2. There are no other biblical examples of women serving in the sanctuary with a lifelong vow of celibacy.

3. Verse 39 is very explicit – Jephthah did to her as he had vowed. And in the 250 occurrences of the mention of burnt offerings, every one of them meant the actual sacrifice being burnt on an altar.

4. An annual commemoration by the daughter's friends would only make sense if she died at the hands of her father. That she might have served in sanctuary for the rest of her life wouldn't demand this kind of lamenting.

Here's the irony of Jephthah's life: With God's help, he triumphed over his enemies, but it was his very dedication to God, that through his rashness and wrong thinking, led him to make a vow that led to personal defeat in the sacrifice of his daughter.

Lessons Learned From the Foolhardiness of Jephthah

1. Be able to separate cultural *values* from Christian *truth*.

The most pressing question that has to be asked in regard to this particular episode is how could a devout follower of Yahweh, the God of the Jews, make and then fulfill a vow that ran contrary to what this same God would desire?

The problem was not his faith – it was pure. The issue was the impact of his *culture* on his *thinking*. You see, Jephthah was a Gileadite. His people were surrounded by the more pervasive Ammonites. During those times, these pagan cultures considered war to be a contest between the gods of their respective nations. (E.g. Elijah advocating Yahweh versus pagan prophets worshipping Baal, 1 Kings 18.) So Jephthah, as a product of his culture, was aligned perfectly with an understanding that the only way he'd win this battle was through the enabling of God. That was okay. He relied on Jewish truth for this part of his battle. The problem came afterward when he made a vow to sacrifice the first person who came out of his house.

His rash promise was based on three faulty premises:

1. **Impulsiveness** – God didn't ask to him to make such a vow; it was an impulsive act based on what he thought was a good intention.

2. **Ecumenism** – He mixed belief in Yahweh with belief in the Moabite god Chemosh, the god of war, whose followers expected a child sacrifice to attain victory in battle.

3. **Assumption** – Once Jephthah made this vow, based on cultural norms, when his daughter came out, he assumed that he had to fulfill it. This was based on wrong thinking, which is exemplified in Numbers 30:2:

"When a man makes a vow to the LORD or takes an oath to obligate himself by a pledge, he must not break his word but must do everything he said."

He believed there was no way out. What he didn't take into account was that it was a greater sin to the Lord to fulfill this vow. Proverbs 26:2: "*An undeserved curse does not come to rest.*"

By the way, a few generations later when Israel finally had its first king, Saul, he too made a rash vow as well, saying that he would put anyone to death who ate before a particular battle. Jonathan, his son, inadvertently ate some honey, and Saul was prepared to fulfill his vow, except the people themselves saved Jonathan:

> "*Saul said, 'May God deal with me, be it ever so severely, if you do not die, Jonathan.'*
>
> *But the men said to Saul, 'Should Jonathan die – he who has brought about this great deliverance in Israel? Never! As surely as the LORD lives, not a hair of his head will fall to the ground, for he did this today with God's help.' So the men rescued Jonathan, and he was not put to death.*"[54]

Jephthah allowed an innocent girl to die because he let his cultural values supersede his faith. We see this same wrong thinking within the church. Certain churches believe that you can only worship God with an organ and a piano, hymnals, and King James Version Bibles. Their belief is based on the premise of *tradition* superseding *modern* culture. Other churches suppose the exact opposite – the only way to worship God is through contemporary means, the rationale being that cultural *relevancy* supersedes *tradition*.

---

[54] 1 Samuel 14:28, 43-45 NIV

It's quite alright to have a particular conviction in regard to living out your faith. The problem is when that conviction undermines and negates another believer, who lives by a different conviction. We're not talking about sinful behavior; we're speaking of an amoral (neither right nor wrong, just different) way of living. We are commanded to read, understand, meditate, and live by Scripture (Psalm 119). But the Bible doesn't say which version of the Bible we are called to read. It is an amoral decision. So choose a King James Version or New International Version Bible or The Message. God doesn't care.

Within my own church, which is Chinese-based, there are differences between the Mandarin-speaking and English-speaking congregations. During the communion, the Mandarin-speaking leadership encourages only those who have been baptized to partake. On the English side, we advocate that baptism is not a prerequisite to participate in the Lord's Supper. The decision on either side is part Scriptural, but also part tradition.

> **The problem is when that conviction undermines and negates another believer who lives by a different conviction.**

In my humble opinion, neither is right nor wrong. The point, however, is that many times our understanding of God and worship and church is influenced by our culture, as much as by Scripture.

To be honest, the above communion example is quite trivial. But bigger battles were fought when believers were not able to differentiate between endemic cultural bias and righteous biblical truth. For example, the Southern Baptist Convention was formed because of a difference of opinion over slavery. The slave culture of the South superseded a biblical understanding that all humans are created in the image of God.

Another example from the recent past was the German Lutherans, who during the 1930s and '40s, hailed Adolf Hitler as their providential national redeemer. Listen to these words:

> "We are full of thanks to God that He, as Lord of history, has given us Adolf Hitler, our leader and savior from our difficult lot. We acknowledge that we, with body and soul, are bound and dedicated to the German state and to its Fuhrer. This bondage and duty contains for us, as evangelical Christians, its deepest and most holy significance in its obedience to the command of God."

Rereading the above passage gives me the creeps. But when you listen to their language, you can tell that these German Lutherans were sincere. However, they were sincerely *wrong*. But that's what happens when you are not able to separate cultural values from Christian truth.

2. God's grace is not dependent upon *self-sacrifice*.

What we mean by this is that God's benevolence, his goodness in enabling us to overcome problems, doesn't call for us to give back to him at the same level. That's an ingrained mentality we all have. When a telemarketer tells you on the phone that you've won a week's vacation free of charge with no obligation, do you believe him? Absolutely not! Why? Because we buy into the belief that, "There's no free lunch." Let me give you a biblical example of this kind of mentality:

The Apostle Paul was a Jewish Christian who became a leading teacher to the Gentiles. In his letter to the Gentile Roman Christians, he explained the theological truth of justification by faith alone apart from being Jew or Gentile. In chapter 9, he revisited his Jewish brothers who were dying without faith in Christ. Romans 9:1-4:

> *"I speak the truth in Christ – I am not lying, my conscience confirms it in the Holy Spirit – I have great sorrow and unceasing anguish in my heart. For I could wish that I myself were cursed and cut off from Christ for the sake of my brothers, those of my own race, the people of Israel."*

What is Paul saying here? On the surface he seems to imply that he would be open to personal damnation if it would bring about the salvation of his people. But Paul just waxed eloquent about justification by faith alone. He knew that God's grace in saving the Jews was not dependent upon him making some grandiose sacrifice. *You can't bargain for God's grace.*

> **You and I can't bargain with God. But Scripture is emphatic that we certainly can ask him for help.**

In our own lives, we need to watch this same kind of mentality. We cannot promise to give God something if he saves a loved one from an incurable disease, or from financial ruin, or even from eternal death.

You and I can't bargain with God. But Scripture is emphatic that we can certainly ask him for help. Paul admonishes us to pray unceasingly (1 Thessalonians 5:17). So prayer is absolutely essential, but like Jephthah, God is not asking us to make a sacrifice commensurate with the level of grace he bestows. If that was the case, our personal salvation would be impossible. There is nothing we can give to or do for God that could earn our salvation. It is a free gift of God. Let's live in God's grace without feeling we have to somehow measure up to it.

3. Don't make *rash* promises to God.

Basically, there are two reasons why we make promises to God: 1) Because of what we've been talking about – we're in trouble, and we bargain with God that, if he'll save us, we'll give back to Him; 2) The other reason is because we truly love God and we want to honor him by rededicating ourselves to a higher level of commitment.

I really appreciate my mentor pastor after I met him coming out of a counseling session with a married couple who was having problems. He said, "Derek, you know, it's so much easier working with youth than it is with adults. With youth, when they're wrong, they feel remorse and desire to change and recommit their lives to God. With adults, they stubbornly cling to their hardheartedness."

Working with youth in the past, I could not agree with him more. I treasure those youth camps where we spend the last evening with kids around a campfire. They come up, hugging one another, confessing their sin, and asking for not only support, but for others to help them transform their lives. They were involved in sexual sin and vowed never to look at pornography again. They'd gossiped against their best friends and vowed never to utter a contemptible word again. They knew they'd shown not only disrespect, but also outright rebellion, and promised to honor their parents from then on.

Let me ask you – how many of these kids do you think kept their vows?

Jesus, in a very well known sermon, had this to say about making a vow to God:

> *"'Again, you have heard that it was said to the people long ago, "Do not break your oath, but keep the oaths you have made to the Lord." But I tell you, do not swear at all: either by heaven, for it is God's throne; or by the earth, for it is his footstool; or by Jerusalem, for it is the city of the Great King. And do not swear by your head, for you cannot make even one hair white or black. Simply let your "Yes" be "Yes," and your "No," "No"; anything beyond this comes from the evil one.'"* [55]

What Jesus is essentially saying is when you make a vow to God, you are required to keep it. The problem is many times, like Jephthah, we haven't thought through what we are vowing to God, and we act impulsively, even with good intentions, and then are forced to renege on our promise. Jesus says don't vow to God. If you want to do something for him, then simply do it. If you want God to save you from something, then simply ask without any strings attached. But remember this: God is good. God is faithful.

---
[55] Matthew 5:33-37 NIV

And when he comes through on his end of the bargain, simply thank him for his benevolence. If only Jephthah would have done the same, he would have enjoyed his latter years, bouncing his grand children on his knees. Let's not make the same mistake as Jephthah:

- *Be able to separate cultural values from Christian truth.*

- *God's grace is not dependent upon self-sacrifice.*

- *Don't make rash promises to God.*

Taking Time to Get Real

Heart-to-Heart

Promises, promises, promises. Think of all the promises you've made to others, even in this last week. You promised your pastor you'd help out with the children's ministry, but you got sidetracked by commitments from your children's school. You promised your wife you'd take care of the kids, but a work project came up unexpectedly. You promised your children a day of fun on Saturday, but had to renege because you promised your friend you'd help them move into a new house.

What do those around you think of your level of commitment? Do you have a reputation of being inconsistent and unreliable?

Why don't you take time right now to confess your lack of dedication in keeping your word? Ask him to not only illuminate those times, but to help you to become a person of your word.

Questions for Discussion

- Recall a recent incident where you broke your promise. How did the person respond? Were they justified in how they felt? How did you feel at the time?

- Did you ever feel like you had to make a promise to God to make him take your heart's desire seriously? Why did you do this and why do you know now this is wrong?

- Have you ever made a vow to God? What was it and why did you feel it was necessary to make at the time?

- What cultural norms have you bought into that seem to collide with biblical truth? Have you ever looked down upon others who did not share your convictions? What does the story of Jephthah show you, in terms of being able to accept others who are different than you?

- What steps can you take in the future to become a person who is known to be reliable and consistent? Why don't you write them down and pray that God would help you fulfill your desire.

Memory Verse: Matthew 5:33-37

Again, you have heard that it was said to the people long ago, "Do not break your oath, but keep the oaths you have made to the Lord." But I tell you, do not swear at all: either by heaven, for it is God's throne; or by the earth, for it is his footstool; or by Jerusalem, for it is the city of the Great King. And do not swear by your head, for you cannot make even one hair white or black. Simply let your "Yes" be "Yes," and your "No," "No"; anything beyond this comes from the evil one.

Heartwork

Take time this week to contact several people who are close to you: your pastor, small group leader, wife, children, parents, boss, etc.

Ask them if they consider you to be a person of your word – reliable, conscientious, and consistent.

Take down their comments and assess whether you need to work on becoming a person of promise.

Samson

No Guarantees
Judges 13:1-14:7

In any given sermon series, there will be an incident or character that is the most well known, the most popular, the one that will be the number one answer on *Family Feud*. If we were asked about the number one incidence recorded in one of the four gospels, it would be Jesus walking on water or the Lord feeding the five thousand with two loaves and five fish. If we were asked about the number one story from the book of Daniel, it would be our hero being protected in the lion's den. A series on the Minor Prophets? Usually the story of Jonah comes to mind, and specifically, the prophet being swallowed by a big fish. From the first book of Genesis? Our survey would probably put Noah and his big boat as the most popular. And from the book of Judges? Hands down, the most famous of the judges, and perhaps the only one that even a biblically illiterate person would be familiar with, is *Samson*.

The Most Famous Judge – Samson

Even those who are vaguely familiar with the biblical Samson character know all about his long hair, his relationship to Delilah, the killing of a lion with his bare hands, and the destruction of the temple when he pushed over the pillars. The story of Samson has always captured the imagination of so many through the ages. But this mighty man of the Old Testament really came on the scene in 1949, when Cecille B. Demille cast Victor Mature as our hero and Hedy Lamarr as the infamous Delilah in his movie epic *Samson and Delilah*. In the 1960s, our hero was introduced to children through a cartoon series from Hanna Barbera called *Young Samson and Goliath*. And in the hip 70s, there was a "blaxploitation" film entitled *Black Samson*, subtitled "Every brother's friend, every mother's enemy."

Unfortunately, because of all this rampant commercialism, Samson has become a caricature, an action-hero-superhunk who makes a great toy for an-eight-year-old boy, but has very little relevance to anyone else. But as I've reviewed the story of Samson, I've found that, if you really dig deep, go beyond the façade of superhuman escapades, you can probably come up with a ten-part series in its own right on how or how not to live. I won't do that, but I want to cover one aspect of Samson's life that I think is very pertinent to each one of us, especially for those of us who have children. To get an idea of where we will be going, we need to get a proper perspective from the time of the judges.

There was at that time this repeated cycle in which the Israelites sinned before God, then in misery, they would cry out for deliverance. God then gives his people a deliverer in the form of a judge, and then they go back to sinning. At the time of Samson, we see this same cycle in Judges 13:1:

> "Again the Israelites did evil in the eyes of the LORD, so the LORD delivered them into the hands of the Philistines for forty years."

Samson – The Beginning

Samson was born during a time when the Israelites were ruled by these judges. *"In those days there was no king in Israel; every man did what was right in his own eyes."*[56] Judges 13:1 tells us that at the time of Samson, the Philistines, a nation originally from the island of Crete, were harassing God's people. They eventually settled in southwest Palestine and were known for their superior iron weapons. Our text further explains that the Jews' oppression was not due to their enemies' advanced weaponry, but rather, to the evil of their own hearts. So God judged the Israelites by handing them over to the Philistines for forty years. But God had compassion, heard their groans, and answers:

> "A certain man of Zorah, named Manoah, from the clan of the Danites, had a wife who was sterile and remained childless. The angel of the LORD appeared to her and said, 'You are sterile and childless, but you are going to conceive and have a son. Now see to it that you drink no wine or other fermented drink and that you do not eat anything unclean, because you will conceive and give birth to a son. No

---
[56] Judges 17:6 NIV

razor may be used on his head, because the boy is to be a Nazirite, set apart to God from birth, and he will begin the deliverance of Israel from the hands of the Philistines.'"[57]

To be childless in that culture was considered a mark of shame. So when God graciously promised a son to Manoah's barren wife, you can imagine how absolutely ecstatic this couple must have been. But as I pondered their incredible good news, I began to wonder, *why this couple?* Why were they chosen, above their peers, to be so blessed? The text doesn't say, but I have to believe, just as in the case of Mary, the mother of Jesus, and Elizabeth, the mother of John the Baptist, that God chose to bless the faithful and righteous.

It was with this understanding in mind that the Lord felt assured of a command he was about to give the mother-to-be:

"The angel of the LORD answered, 'Your wife must do all that I have told her. She must not eat anything that comes from the grapevine, nor drink any wine or other fermented drink nor eat anything unclean. She must do everything I have commanded her.'"[58]

"Mrs. Manoah, don't consume alcohol, nor eat anything non-kosher, because your son will be a Nazirite." Nazirite, you say? The parents understood this to mean that their son was to be separated and consecrated exclusively to the Lord.

---

[57] Judges 17:2-5 NIV
[58] Judges 17:13-14 NIV

Normally in those days, a person chose to be a Nazirite by making a vow before and to God to separate him- or herself from worldly things and to consecrate, set themselves apart, for God's work. Typically, Nazirites would keep these vows for a prescribed thirty days, or a double period of sixty days, or even triple time of ninety to one hundred days. Samson was called, however, a "Nazirite for life," just like the prophet Samuel and, later, John the Baptist, the forerunner to Jesus. Before any of them were born, their vows were taken for them by their parents.

It is an important crux to our story to remember that Nazirites agreed to abstain from wine and other intoxicating drinks, and they refused to cut their hair, including shaving, because the purpose of their long tresses were to serve as a visible sign of the Nazirite's consecration to the Lord.[59] Finally, a Nazirite also refused to touch or go near a dead body because this would make him/her ceremonially unclean. Note that the angel asked Samson's mother to keep these same vows during her pregnancy. And as a godly and devout woman, she completely obeyed.

As godly and concerned parents-to-be, Manoah and his wife asked the angel how to raise the boy:

> *"O Lord, I beg you, let the man of God you sent to us come again to teach us how to bring up the boy who is to be born."*[60]

In addition, Manoah sought to honor God by offering a young goat and grain offering to the Lord. In every way,

---

[59] E.g. Numbers 6:7
[60] Judges 13:8 NIV

this devout couple showed themselves to be faithful. We skip ahead to nine months later:

> *"The woman gave birth to a boy and named him Samson. He grew and the LORD blessed him, and the Spirit of the LORD began to stir him while he was in Mahaneh Dan, between Zorah and Eshtaol."*[61]

These passages tell us a lot about the relationship between Manoah's family and God. You might look at your own family background, be envious, and say, "I never had it so good!" And it may be true. Compare Samson's upbringing with Jephthah, an earlier judge, who was born to a prostitute. Jephthah was unloved and unwelcomed by his own brothers and people. Jephthah was never given a chance to reach his full potential. And then we look at Samson. He had every advantage you could imagine – his birth was predicted by an angel, he had godly parents who loved Yahweh, and he was uniquely set apart for God's work. Verse 24 rightly affirms that this boy was blessed by God. Further, verse 25 assures that God's Holy Spirit stirred in him. That term *"to stir"* is the strongest action spoken of by the Spirit of God. It was used of Pharoah[62] and Nebuchadnezzar,[63] when it spoke of them having dreams from God. God himself was stirring up within young Samson a desire and a heart to fulfill his role as deliverer of his people. His whole life is being directed and nurtured to do great

---

[61] Judges 13:24-25 NIV
[62] Genesis 41:8 NIV
[63] Daniel 2:1, 3 NIV

things. Unfortunately, we find a slight detour to the great plan beginning in chapter 14:1-2:

> *"Samson went down to Timnah and saw there a young Philistine woman. When he returned, he said to his father and mother, 'I have seen a Philistine woman in Timnah; now get her for me as my wife.'"*

Let's pick up the context for this passage. The Philistines have now controlled this territory for four decades. Unlike previous conquerors, the Philistines have been more "benevolent" than previous subjugators. This allowed an Israelite like Samson to travel freely four miles southwest from his home town to Timnah. It was there that he was captivated by a Philistine woman. We don't know her name, but we know what she looked like...drop dead gorgeous! It was love at first sight...and it is here we get our initial insight into the foundation of Samson's many problems. He was a man controlled by his sensual desires, by his passion.

But Manoah and his wife perhaps recalled their earlier days. They were once teenagers, too. They knew puppy love when they saw it.

I recall sharing a concern with an elderly pastor of a young teen who had a strong infatuation for a pretty girl. With wise insight he said to me, "It may be puppy love, but to the puppy, it's very real."

This is not exactly the answer Samson's parents would have wanted to hear. We pick up their response in Judges 14:3:

> "His father and mother replied, 'Isn't there an acceptable woman among your relatives or among all our people? Must you go to the uncircumcised Philistines to get a wife?'"

Being godly parents and very wise in their understanding of God's ways, Manoah and his wife realized quickly that this Philistine wasn't the right woman for Samson. There were two reasons: 1) she wasn't from their relatives, or even their clan; 2) as a Philistine, she would have worshipped foreign gods.

For those of us living in 21st century America, the thought of parents having such influence or control over the lives of their adult children seems so foreign. We've been taught by our society that we make our own decisions. All others, including our teachers, pastors, and even parents need to butt out! Times have certainly changed because, in the era of the judges, it was the parents' responsibility to pick a wife for their son or, at the very least, to have a significant say in the matter.

And how did our hero respond to their admonition?

> "But Samson said to his father, 'Get her for me. She's the right one for me.'"[64]

Put into our modern-day vernacular, Samson essentially was saying to his parents, "She's the one I want and that's it! No *if*, *ands*, or *buts* about it!" What parent hasn't heard or

---
[64] Judges 14:3b NIV

felt the same attitude from his/her child? When we are confronted so directly by our children, we as parents have a decision to make – put our foot down, "It's my way or the highway!" or compromise, "Okay, son, we'll help you out."

A Personal Example

When I was a teen, my friend got a motocross bike from his parents. And of course, I had to have one myself. I think my dad was open to the idea, but my mom was Gibraltar, immoveable on her eldest getting a dirt bike and killing himself. She didn't spend all that time raising me up, only to bury me even before I left the house. Her answer was an emphatic, "No!" It was a non-negotiable.

> **When we are confronted so directly by our children, we as parents have a decision to make – put our foot down, or compromise**

Now compare that with an incident that happened a few years earlier. I remember growing up with my two siblings; we were a meat-eating family. No salads or vegetables for us. It was always steak, pork chops, or fried chicken. But one time, my parents decided to cook us liver. Sitting at the dinner table, it was unanimous that none of us wanted to eat this weird-textured grossness. My parents threatened us. "You eat the liver or you won't be allowed to leave the table until it's gone!"

Five o'clock became six o'clock, then seven and eight. Finally at 9:00 p.m., the meat was still untouched, and my parents resigned themselves to the fact that we wouldn't eat liver. After that night, they never served it to us again. That was an incident of compromise. It wasn't worth fighting over.

Samson's parents realized that they had to pick their battles, and in this case, even though they knew it was a wrong choice, they nevertheless went down to Timnah with Samson to work out the marriage arrangements:

> "Samson went down to Timnah together with his father and mother. As they approached the vineyards of Timnah, suddenly a young lion came roaring toward him. The Spirit of the LORD came upon him in power so that he tore the lion apart with his bare hands as he might have torn a young goat. But he told neither his father nor his mother what he had done. Then he went down and talked with the woman, and he liked her."[65]

I read this passage and every time I visualize it: Samson is some ancient Hebrew Arnold Schwarzeneggar-type of dude with biceps larger than my thighs. But if you read the text carefully, it says nothing about his physical strength. It does mention that he accomplished this incredible feat of killing a lion with his bare hands because the Spirit of God came upon him. For all we know, he could have been a 98-lb. weakling, a cross between Steve Urkel and Don Knotts.[66] The lesson for us here is that true strength is not based on

---

[65] Judges 14:5-7 NIV
[66] For those of you who are television illiterate, Urkel was a geeky character from the '90s sitcom *Family Matters*. For those of you who are older, you might remember Don Knotts played Deputy Barney Fife in the '60s comedy *The Andy Griffith Show*.

our physical might or mental prowess, but rather, true power that finds its foundation in our spiritual connectedness to Christ.

Now there's something else in this text that hints of another aspect of Samson's character. Note that his parents knew nothing about this incident with the lion. Perhaps they took a different route than their son (verses 8 – 9). It was during this brief interlude that Samson broke two of his vows as a Nazirite: 1) He went to a vineyard and took of the grapes (i.e. he consumed alcohol); and 2) He killed the lion (i.e. he came into contact with a dead body).

Spiritually, he was ceremonially unclean, but his parents were unaware of his defilement. And it was this hidden sin that kept Samson on the wrong path. The awful truth is that sin finds its greatest strength in darkness. Rather than tell his parents, Samson hid his sin and the sin pushed him farther down the wrong path. Judges 14:7 says that he went down to Timnah and met with the Philistine woman again and, thus, reinforced his desire. What those of us who are familiar with Samson know is that when you play with fire, you'll eventually get burned.

> **The awful truth is that sin finds its greatest strength in darkness.**

A Lesson Learned From a Biblical He-Man

So begins our exploration into the psychological, spiritual, and mental psyche of Samson. As we come to the close of this chapter, we can ask, "What can we learn from his life that we can apply to ours?"

I think as a parent, I realize from the life of Samson that there are no guarantees that my child will become an outstanding person.

Think with me on Samson's background. Aren't most of us on the same wavelength with Manoah and his wife? We eagerly seek to have children. As devout Christians, we desire to raise them in the Lord. We direct them in their studies to excel in school, and we nurture their spiritual disciplines to develop good character and a devotion to God. We pray that they would find a good spouse, one who loves the Lord. We do everything in our power for all these things to happen, and those darn kids...they take the wrong path!

> There are no guarantees that my child will become an outstanding person.

And it's not like we weren't prepared to do it right. When a child of promise is given to us by the Lord, we look to our own parents for advice. We even use their negative example and strive not to do to our children what was done to us. We read books from leading child psychologists and pediatricians – to spank or not to spank – give grace, administer discipline. We pore over information on baby websites. We purchase every known gizmo and gadget to aid in raising our kids properly. We avoid violence on TV, or better yet, have no TV in the house. We watch our language around them. We move to new locations and take up new jobs so that our kids can be in the best school systems with the best teachers while living in the best neighborhoods. We involve ourselves in their academic studies, music practice, and athletic endeavors. We pray with them at meals and over them when they go to sleep. We encourage them to keep their quiet times and help them with their Awana projects. We do all these things and send them off to college, praying that they would stay close to the Lord, work hard on their studies, avoid making foolish choices, associate with peers of good character, get into a godly relationship, find a meaningful job, and be able to do well financially. And darn those kids...they take all our effort and mess up!

And their foibles aren't a secret, are they? You hear the whispering among those in your fellowship, the snickering around you in the pews, and the disapproving glances at PTA meetings about how your child is a bad egg. Must be his/her upbringing; the parents weren't involved enough. You know what they say, "The nut doesn't fall far from the tree!" And you want to shout from the pews, yell from your rooftop, shake a few people up, "It's not our fault! We've done everything in our power to raise our children right!"

And you know what? God hears from above, and he says, "Yes, it's not your fault." You have done the best that you can, and I honor your effort. But you need to swallow your pride, humble yourself, and realize that your child is not some pet project. It is not as simple as answering correctly, pressing all the right buttons, and, voila, expecting a model child to come out.

God's Encouragement for Us

God says, "You see, I made your child unique. His DNA is as original as an individual snowflake, as distinct as his fingerprints. If you read my owner's manual, you'll note that I created his inmost being. I knit him together in the womb. He/is fearfully and wonderfully made."[67] And you need to realize, like God's chosen servant Abraham to his beloved son Isaac, that your child was given to you by him; he doesn't belong to you – he belongs to God.

Sometimes we need that gentle reminder that A + B doesn't necessarily equal C...especially when it comes to bringing up kids. I find it interesting and ironic that the parents who are the most apt to tell you how raise your children have the most messed up kids. They just don't see it because they're living in this dream world where their children do everything right. But the problem is, like what Samson did to his parents in the vineyard, their children keep things from them. They live two different lives – the one around the home and church, and the other at school and among their friends. And you say to yourself, "Why? We have an open and honest relationship. I treat him/her with respect. Why do I see a different child than what everyone else sees?"

> **Your child was given to you by me; he doesn't belong to you – he belongs to me."**

The reason is expectations. Your child knows what you expect, and he knows you couldn't handle what they: a) really want to be; and b) really are. So they keep things from you and show you a perfect façade. And you get to live the continual fantasy of a perfect family, having the model child. That's what Samson did in the vineyard when he killed that lion. He kept his sin from his parents, and sin always finds its strength in darkness. It gets more and more powerful with each passing day of secrecy. Don't believe it? Ask the

---

[67] Adapted from Psalm 139:13-14

guy struggling with internet porn or homosexual urges; think of the wife who has been cheating on her husband for months, or the husband who's addicted to gambling.

Samson, steeped in sin, went down the path of destruction, re-hooked up with the Philistine babe, a woman who was absolutely no good for him. *Question:* But what can you do as a parent of an adult child? *Answer:* Nothing. A counseling professor in my seminary asked us as a class if our children have a right to choose hell. The answer is, of course, yes. As parents, we can't save them from hell. It is ultimately their choice to choose Jesus or to reject him. We learn this lesson from Samson. No matter how much effort we put in, there are no absolute guarantees.

What Can We Do?

So in the end of this chapter on Samson, we come away not feeling very good about all the effort we've put into raising our children, right? What else can we do?

The answer is reflected in our understanding that we are not in control of our children, God is. We need to be involved, we need to give and sacrifice, we need to set a good example, but most importantly, we need to *pray*. We need to get on our hands and knees daily, lift up our children on our family altar, and ask God to mold them into the kind of vessels he cherishes and can use. Don't pray that they won't ever stumble because we all stumble. But

> **We need to be involved, we need to give and sacrifice, we need to set a good example, but most importantly, we need to *pray*.**

rather, pray that, when they do take a wrong turn, they might learn from their mistakes and get back on the right path. And when God brings them back toward home, pray for humility. Pray that when your little one comes back, you won't chastise, you won't begin with an "I told you so," but rather, like the father of the Prodigal, just embrace them with open arms, and say, "Welcome back."

That's for you to do, whether you're a Manoah and/or a Mrs. Manoah. But perhaps, you're not quite there in your life. You're either married and don't have children, or you're single. You identify more with Samson than with his parents. There's a lesson for you as well.

Be thankful that, even though your parents are far from perfect in character and in raising you, they've done the absolute best job that they could do. Yes, they wanted you to do well in school and often pushed you, like maybe poor Samson when he was young, to excel above all the rest. And maybe you grew up with the feeling of pressure not just at home, but at church as well. It seems like all your Sunday School teachers, youth leaders, and pastors seem to care about is that you know the right answer and that you behave properly. And you felt like there's got to be more to Christianity than a bunch of Dos and Don'ts. "Hey, it may be good for my parents, but it's not my religion!" And so, you have a deep resentment for the hypocrisy you see and the shallowness of the faith. And like Samson, you want to rebel. You want to rip some lion apart.

If that's where your heart is right now, God has a message for you, too, and it's this: Your heavenly Father doesn't give letter grades for what you know or what you don't know. He's not standing in the corner waiting to pounce on you for what you do or don't do. He's not going to send a note home to your parents or nag you about keeping your devotions. Do you know what God cares about?

He cares about you!

He cares that you truly seek to have a personal and vital relationship with Him. Do you care for the same?

Taking Time to Get Real

Heart-to-Heart

For those who have children...

Scripture tells us that our children are fearfully and wonderfully made. For you and your idea of children, *fear* might be a better descriptor than *wonderful*. Take out a sheet of paper and, for each of your children, write down all the wonderful qualities they possess. Don't just focus on their accomplishments, also write of their temperament, personality – the intangibles. On a second piece of paper, write out various past events or times where they brought you joy, laughter, and a sense of pride. End the time by praying and thanking God for your children.

For those who are single...

Take this chapter to reflect by putting yourself in the role of Samson. Perhaps upon self-evaluation, you are disappointed with how things have turned out, the wrong decisions you've made in life, the disappointment you face because you don't feel blessed by God. But Scripture tells us you are fearfully and wonderfully made. This may be uncomfortable, but take out a piece of paper and write down all the wonderful qualities you possess. Write down your accomplishments and the positive qualities of your personality and temperament. On a second piece of paper, assuming that you would desire to have children someday, write a letter to them explaining these qualities that you'd like to pass onto them. Pray to the Lord that he would bring you the right mate and that you might raise up godly children. Remember, finding the perfect mate first means *becoming* the perfect mate.

Questions for Discussion

- Whether you grew up in a godly Christian home or not, discuss how your parents succeeded and failed in raising you and your siblings.

- Would you consider yourself to be more strong-willed or compliant in personality? (Note: neither description is necessarily negative or positive.) How has that shaped who you've become?

- What qualities do you see in Samson that are reflected in yourself? How have those qualities manifested themselves in your life?

- If you've been one who has had previous relationships in the past, describe the wrong attitudes and decisions you had with those individuals.

- How would you describe the depth of your intercessory prayer for your children? Do you think the fervency, or lack thereof, has affected the decisions your children have made and what they have become?

- If you were only allowed to give one piece of advice to your children, what would you love to pass on?

Memory Verse: 1 John 2:15-17

Do not love the world or anything in the world. If anyone loves the world, the love of the Father is not in him. For everything in the world – the cravings of sinful man, the lust of his eyes and the boasting of what he has and does – comes not from the Father but from the world. The world and its desires pass away, but the man who does the will of God lives forever.

Heartwork

Determine a time in the future that you will fast and pray for your children. Pray that God would take a hold of their lives and that you would be the positive, godly influence needed to move them in the right direction.

If you are single, please pray for how God can work in your life to overcome your personal failures. In terms of fasting, ask the Lord when and how long you should continue to fast.

Note: remember to check with your physician to see if fasting is okay for you.

Barnabas

Loving the Loser
Acts 15:35-39

You may have been valedictorian in your high school or one of the top graduates in your engineering class at your university. You may have won awards for your trumpet or piano playing or ball-handling abilities. You may have been voted as the best employee or best manager at your company. But I can bet that, no matter how good you were or are, there has been a time in your life when you blew it. And I'm not talking about making some little mistake, like striking the wrong key during a piano recital or making a free throw that rimmed out and cost your team the game. I mean an ultimate, no holds bar, royal mess up, the kind that negatively affects the outcome of your life, the kind that leads people to think of you as a total loser.

The Desire for Success

We all crave success. We all want to prove that we're competent, and when called upon to do something of consequence, will accomplish it with flying colors. But let's face it; it's not realistic to be perfect. If you're a doctor, your misdiagnosis is buried. If you're a lawyer, your poor defense gets put behind bars. A dentist's mistakes are pulled. A businessman's poor decision ends up in red ink. An engineer's miscalculations crash. And pastor's mistakes? Pastors don't make mistakes. We're God's anointed! No, of course pastors make mistakes. When pastors make mistakes, *people fall away from the faith.*

We all make mistakes. We all blow it. Back in 1957, Henry Ford bragged about creating the "car of the decade." That was the Edsel. How bad was this car? One business writer likened the Edsel's sales graph to a steep ski slope. He added that, as far as he knew, there was only one case on record of an Edsel ever being stolen.

A Biblical Loser – John Mark

Actually, the Bible is replete with losers: Cain, Pharoah, all the Kings of Israel. The one we want to focus on is a young man whose parents gave him the Hebrew name, John. But you may recognize him by his Latin name, Marcus, or Mark. It's difficult to think of this guy, John Mark, as a loser since he was born into a wealthy family and hung around of lot of Christian VIPs at the time. There's no mention of his father, which we can assume that he died earlier, but his mother Mary owned a mansion in Jerusalem, complete with servants (Acts 12:12). Mary was very prominent in the Christian community in Jerusalem; in fact, the church met in her home (Luke 12:12-13).

Having such a head start in life, coming from a prominent family, and having wealth, John Mark would hardly be labeled as a loser. But let me describe his situation to you, and you make a judgment for yourself.

Three Reasons Why John Mark is a Loser

Reason #1 – The First Ever Streaker

First of all, we see his loser-like qualities the first time we're introduced to him in the Bible. It was when Jesus was still alive, on the night when our Lord spent his final hours in an upper room in Jerusalem, comforting his beloved disciples. Leaving the city at night, they went out the gates of Jerusalem across the Kidron Valley up to the Mount of Olives. There Jesus prayed for comfort from the Father, knowing that the one disciple missing from his group, Judas, would be coming at any moment with a legion of Roman soldiers to betray him. Jesus rebuked his disciples for falling asleep instead of keeping guard.

We pick up the introduction of Mark in the story at this point in the narrative. Maybe he had heard the commotion of Jesus and the disciples from his room when they left the city. In any case, he put on a nightshirt and followed the disciples up to the Mount of Olives. We pick up the story in Mark 14:51-52, where the Roman soldiers approach Jesus:

> "*A young man, wearing nothing but a linen garment, was following Jesus. When they seized him, he fled naked, leaving his garment behind.*"

Even though he isn't given a name (would you want to be identified if this happened to you?), scholars believe this young man to be John Mark. Back in the 1970s, there were people who would run around naked in public. They were called "streakers." Evidently, their purpose was to cause a stir within an unexpecting crowd. Streakers were intentional in their nakedness. John Mark's streaking, however, was unintentional. Now granted, the other disciples fled as well. But John Mark is the only one who gets his clothes ripped off and runs away naked. LOSER!

Reason #2 – Missed Opportunity

So John Mark's a loser because he was caught fleeing the scene naked. Another way that John marked himself as a loser was because he didn't take advantage of being around such prominent Christians. What do I mean by this?

His mother's home was a magnet for the Christian community. Apostles, prophets, church planters and prominent evangelists all came by the house because it was the place to be. At an early age, Mark with acquainted with leaders such as James and John, two of Jesus' key disciples. He knew James, the half-brother of Jesus, who shepherded the church in Jerusalem. He probably talked to Simon Peter, the lead disciple of Jesus, on a frequent basis, as well as the Apostle Paul, the greatest missionary, church planter, and theologian in the history of the church. Then of course there was Barnabas, John Mark's cousin. I'm sure Barnabas came by for dinner on a regular basis. So here are all these prominent leaders, pillars of the faith, and we don't get a sense from John Mark's early days that they had much impact on him.

To understand what the equivalent would be like now, try to picture living in a home where Dr. James Dobson, Pastor Rick Warren, and Rev. Billy Graham would come by on a frequent basis. I would hope that being around such prominence would cause me to want to excel as well. But I don't see it in John Mark. He was more like a groupie, a person who got his sense of self worth through being with others. He hung around great men, but did not, himself, take advantage of it. A missed *opportunity* is as bad as making a *mistake*. That, in my opinion, makes him a loser.

> **A missed *opportunity* is as bad as making a *mistake*.**

Reason #3 – Mama's Boy

There's one more reason why John Mark was a loser. It occurred when his cousin Barnabas and the Apostle Paul were called on by the church to go on a missionary journey. Acts 12:25:

> *"When Barnabas and Saul had finished their mission, they returned from Jerusalem, taking with them John, also called Mark."*

Why did they bring Mark? Acts 13:5 tells us that, *"When they arrived at Salamis, they proclaimed the word of God in the Jewish synagogues. John was with them as their helper."*

I believe that Barnabas and Paul saw bringing Mark along on their journey as an opportunity for discipleship.

Here was a young man who had been clinging to his mother's apron strings all his life, while they'd been out, making an impact for the Kingdom of God. They desired to bring him along to give him a taste of what was out there. The text tells us that he served the Apostles in the capacity of "assistant," a somewhat lofty term, which simply meant he was a "go-fer," probably involved with things like making arrangements for travel, buying food, and finding lodging.

Things were going well for a while, but then Paul decided to go back to Perga to confirm the work of the churches that he established on his first journey. Something happened to John Mark at this point:

> *"From Paphos, Paul and his companions sailed to Perga in Pamphylia, where John left them to return to Jerusalem."*[68]

The text doesn't tell us why John Mark left the disciples stranded without assistance. It just says that he went back to Jerusalem. Perhaps because of his young age or immaturity, he couldn't hack it on the road. Maybe he didn't like the food, or he wasn't used to being around so many Gentiles. Maybe he was afraid of highway bandits, or maybe he was just plain homesick and wanted to be back with his mother.

We don't know his reason for leaving. But being a "bottom-line" type of guy, the Apostle Paul now designated John Mark as a flake. He couldn't be trusted. He wasn't dependable. I can just hear Paul dialoguing with Barnabas for the rest of the missionary trip. "That cousin of yours...I can't believe he deserted us like this! How can we do the work of the Lord when people flake out? I'll never trust him again."

---

[68] Acts 13:13 NIV

We see this attitude evidenced two years later, when Paul and Barnabas decided to strike out on a second missionary journey:

> *"Some time later Paul said to Barnabas, 'Let us go back and visit the brothers in all the towns where we preached the word of the Lord and see how they are doing.' Barnabas wanted to take John, also called Mark, with them, but Paul did not think it wise to take him, because he had deserted them in Pamphylia and had not continued with them in the work. They had such a sharp disagreement that they parted company."*[69]

While I deeply admire the Apostle Paul for his multifaceted gifting by the Lord for his kingdom work, we get a glimpse of his temperament from his writings in the New Testament. He obviously had a strong personality with a kind of "my way or the highway" sort of mentality. He saw John Mark as undependable, a man who just couldn't cut it. So the Apostle Paul wanted to cut him out.

Our text ends with Paul and Barnabas in sharp disagreement over the matter. The word in the Greek, when used in a negative context as in this case, connotes anger, a stirring up of emotions. Barnabas and Paul were literally going toe to toe on this matter. Now, can you imagine poor John Mark in the middle of this situation? He knew he blew it deserting these two back in Pamphylia. I'm sure when the Apostle Paul got back to his mother's house, Mark avoided him like the plague. The glaring eyes, the imperceptible shaking of the Apostle Paul's head probably didn't elude

---

[69] Acts 15:36-39 NIV

John Mark. And now, he had to listen to his cousin standing up for him to the great Apostle Paul. How embarrassing! How shameful!

It's during times like these when we all have to make a decision on what direction we will head in our faith – forward or backward. We can't become dejected, feel a sense of hopelessness, and decide, "It's just not worth it! I don't want to do great things for the Lord any more. I've tried and failed. The Lord can't use a failure like me. The Father doesn't want losers serving in his kingdom." I can imagine John Mark feeling this way, his feelings of inferiority pervading his soul.

> It's during times like these when we all have to make a decision on what direction we will head in our faith – forward or backward.

Speaking of inferior, a story is told of a man who paid a visit to his local psychologist. When the doctor asked what had prompted the visit, the man said, "I'm suffering from an inferiority complex."

In the ensuing weeks, the psychologist put his new patient through an intensive battery of tests. Next came the long wait, while the test results were tabulated and appropriate correlations were made. Finally, the doctor called the man and asked him to return to the clinic. "I have some interesting news for you," the doctor began.

"What's that?" asked the man.

"It's no complex," the psychologist reported, "You are inferior."

You are Inferior!

Ouch! John Mark most likely felt inferior; he felt like a loser. He had been rejected by the greatest Christian minister in his day, and what's more, his own cousin was defending him. I love my mom, but when I get in a dispute with another person, I don't want her defending me. It's embarrassing. Perhaps it was the same for John Mark.

John Mark suffers from Charlie Brown syndrome. With Lucy holding the football, old Charlie never thinks he'll be able to kick it. He's a loser, and once a loser, always a loser. The only problem with that kind of thinking is that, if you decide to stay a loser, then you are a loser.

But I praise God that that's not how our faith works. Our heavenly Father takes the weak things of this world and molds and shapes them to be used for his purpose. If we assume that John Mark can't overcome, then we don't understand our faith. We've made the wrong assumptions.

In the book *The Incomplete Book of Failures*,[70] here are some gems by people who made some wrong assumptions about others:

> **Our heavenly Father takes the weak things of this world and molds and shapes them to be used for his purpose.**

> *"Far too noisy, my dear Mozart. Far too many notes."*
> The Emperor Ferdinand after the first performance of the Marriage of Figaro

---

[70] Pile, Stephen, The (Incomplete) Book of Failures: The Official Handbook of the Not-Terribly-Good Club of Great Britain, 1979

> "If Beethoven's Seventh Symphony is not by some means abridged, it will soon fall into disuse."
> Philip Hale, Boston music critic, 1837

> "Rembrandt is not to be compared in the painting of character with our extraordinarily gifted English artist Mr. Rippingille."
> John Hunt (1775 – 1848)

> "Flight by machines heavier than air is impractical and insignificant...utterly impossible."
> Simon Newcomb (1835 – 1909)

> "We don't like their sound. Groups of guitars are on their way out."
> Decca Recording Company when turning down the Beatles in 1962

> "You will never amount to very much."
> A Munich schoolmaster to Albert Einstein, age 10

Barnabas, John Mark's older cousin, understood the notion of *faith* overcoming *failure*. We witness this man of encouragement lift up a discouraged brother:

> "Barnabas took Mark and sailed for Cyprus, but Paul chose Silas and left, commended by the brothers to the grace of the Lord."[71]

---

[71] Acts 15:39b-40 NIV

In actually, because of Barnabas' encouragement, which was demonstrated in coming alongside Mark, it was better for the gospel, because now there were two missionary groups instead of one going out to do the Lord's work.

The Results of Encouragement

Barnabas was a man who saw beyond the externals. He was a man who was able to see to the heart of the matter. Perhaps both Paul and Barnabas were right in their assessment of John Mark. Paul was right in assessing that it may have been too soon for Mark to venture out. But Barnabas certainly was right in that he correctly ascertained that there was good raw material in his cousin Mark. Because Mark had lost his father, Barnabas came alongside him and became a father figure to this young man. He supported him. He believed in him.

We began this chapter by noting what a failure John Mark was when he was younger. But I don't think it would be too far off to say that, because of Barnabas' encouragement at his lowest point, John Mark was able to get back in the proverbial saddle again. This young man went on to do some extraordinary things.

I Love You, Man!

Because Barnabas brought Mark along with him on his journey, and the mission was a success, the Apostle Paul later realized how valuable, trustworthy, and dependable Mark could be. This break between Paul and Barnabas occurred about A.D. 49-50, and John Mark was not heard from again until a decade later. We first hear of him again, interestingly enough, by Paul and, I might add, in favorable terms. In his letter to Philemon, Paul asks his friend to receive Mark with a welcome, no longer as an assistant but as one of his "fellow laborers."[72] And during his imprisonment in Rome, Paul tells Timothy to bring Mark with him to Rome, "...*for he is useful to me for ministry.*"[73]

John Mark repaired his relationship with the Apostle Paul. But he developed an even more intimate relationship with the Apostle Peter. Look at how Peter referred to him at the end of his first letter:

> "*She who is in Babylon, chosen together with you, sends you her greetings, and so does my son Mark.*"[74]

He calls John Mark his son! Obviously there is some affection between them. Mark took to the older man very early on and became his personal assistant, interpreter, and secretary in Rome. It was through his relationship with Peter, where he heard the Apostle retell the stories over and over again, that he made one of the greatest impacts on our faith – he wrote the first gospel which bears his name, *The Gospel of Mark*. Of the four gospels, it was the first ever written, and Luke and Matthew borrowed from Mark's letter in writing their own gospels.

The church historian Eusebius wrote later that Mark was the first evangelist sent to Egypt and was the founder of the

---

[72] Philemon 24 NIV
[73] 2 Timothy 4:11 NIV
[74] 1 Peter 5:13 NIV

churches in Alexandria, where he was made the first bishop of the city. So great were his converts, both in number and sincerity of commitment, says Eusebius, that the great Jewish philosopher, Philo, was amazed.

With a Little Bit of Encouragement

Mark could have been permanently devastated by the mistrust of the Apostle Paul against him at the beginning of their second missionary journey. He could have washed out and became a nobody, making absolutely no impact for our faith. But a man named Barnabas, the son of encouragement, came alongside him and showed that he believed in the young man, and that was enough to help Mark get back on his own two feet and do something great for the faith, the writing of his gospel.

You could be a Barnabas to someone else who is young in the faith. Maybe he feels like a loser. Maybe he feels like nothing he does for Jesus will ever amount to much. Would you be willing to come alongside one such as him and help him believe not only in himself, but also in the possibility that God can use him greatly?

> **You could be a Barnabas to someone else who is young in the faith.**

The Impact of Encouragement – Personal Testimony

I would like to share my testimony of my call to ministry. It was in 1986, on a vacation fishing trip with my family.

That fall, I was about to start a Master's program in Business at Santa Clara University in California, believing the Lord was desiring for me to further my business career. However on this trip, I distinctly felt the impression that the Lord wanted me to consider full-time pastoral ministry.

I went back to my home church, and my pastor said, "Let's test out the call. Why don't you become an intern in the church?" I was so excited about the fact that God was calling me to pastoral ministry that I eventually enrolled in seminary, pursuing both graduate programs concurrently. At the church, I was moved from interning with the Young Adult Fellowship to serving in our high school ministry. The church was satisfied with my progress and so my pastor asked me to move to the college ministry, where I would work directly under him. The plan was that there would be a transition time where I would eventually be asked to take over this ministry. I had the greatest joy knowing that I was eventually going to be a pastor in my own home church.

Within the college ministry, I implemented an outreach program on the campus of both Cal-State University, Hayward, and Chabot Community College. I was in charge of follow up, and led Bible studies and Sunday School. I ran various camps and activities. After six months, I asked my pastor when the transition would begin. He said, "Not yet," so I continued in my ministries. After six more months, I asked him again when the transition would take place. He said that he wasn't sure. Finally after another six months, I asked him what was happening. He took me over to our senior pastor's office and the two of them, with a combined seventy years of pastoral ministry, sat down with me. I remember the meeting quite vividly. They were both trying to be encouraging, but the bottom line was that they didn't see the pastoral gift in me. They thought I might make a great Bible teacher within a Christian high school or Bible college, but they didn't see me as a pastor in a church.

Suffice to say, I was crushed. My whole world collapsed around me. I was so sure that I was called to pastor, but how could I ignore two men, whom I greatly admired and whose opinions I deeply respected. What was I to do? I found out later that I wasn't called to do anything. I would need to trust God to make his plans clear.

I Got By With a Little Help from My Friends

A seminarian friend from Sacramento, California, asked me to speak at his youth camp. These were Chinese kids, and even though I am Chinese by descent, I had never spoken to Chinese before. The age range was from junior high to college, 150 students in all. I prayed about it, and to make a long story short, God opened up this new ministry for me. What was most encouraging, however, was that the collegians from that camp came down the next Thursday and made the two-hour trip to visit my college fellowship. After meeting them, my pastor came up to me and said, "You know, Derek, you are called to pastor, it's just in a different ministry context." I could live with that!

Those collegians who came to visit me in my home church were like Barnabas for me. When I was at my lowest, their presence made me realize that God, indeed, wanted to use me. And now, I've been serving at a Chinese church since 1993. Lord willing, he will allow me to continue to serve him as he sees fit.

There may be someone that you can encourage to keep on keeping on. Why don't you ask the Lord this morning to bring to mind that one individual who feels like a loser, but needs to be reminded that he/she is important to God.

Taking Time to Get Real

Heart-to-Heart

In this chapter, you have one or two characters with which you can identify: John Mark or Barnabas.

John Mark

You may be identifying more with John Mark right now. You feel like the poster child for a book on Murphy's Law. Right now, you need some encouragement! Do you believe God's Word? Do you believe it when it says you are fearfully and wonderfully made?[75] Do you believe that you're God's workmanship created in Christ Jesus to do good work?[76] Why don't you pray to the Lord to help you see yourself as God sees you? Don't let Satan or those around make you believe you're useless.

Barnabas

Think of those in your life who need to be encouraged — a spouse, a child, your parent, a coworker, a neighbor, or a friend at church. Identify different ways that you might bring cheer into their lives. Maybe it's writing a note or sending an email. It could be a phone call or taking them out to lunch. You figure it out, and now the most important thing…do it!

---

[75] Psalm 139:14 NIV
[76] Ephesians 2:10 NIV

Questions for Discussion

- Describe an incident or situation where you utterly failed. What were the ramifications of your failure? How did it affect you and those around you?

- In spite of feeling like a failure, come up with a few examples of how you succeeded. If you have difficulty in recalling them, ask a close friend to remind you of your successes.

- Think of a person in your life who is like Barnabas, a person who knows how to encourage. How has this person encouraged you?

- Do you know of any specific person who could use your encouragement right now? How would you go about encouraging him/her?

- Barnabas demonstrated loyalty to John Mark. Can you recall a time when someone stood by you, even though it might have caused them embarrassment? How about a time when you stood by someone who needed you?

- Share a verse that has brought you encouragement. Is there an instance right now where that same verse could encourage another?

Memory Verse: Philippians 1:3-6

I thank my God every time I remember you. In all my prayers for all of you, I always pray with joy because of your partnership in the gospel from the first day until now, being confident of this, that he who began a good work in you will carry it on to completion until the day of Christ Jesus.

Heartwork

Put some of these things into practice this week:

- When you feel like being critical of your family member, instead, write down ten things that you are thankful for with regard to your spouse or your child(ren).
- Say, "I love you," everyday, but add the reason for it. "I love you because…"
- Say, "I'm proud of you every day, but add the reason for it. "I'm proud of you for…"
- Within your fellowship/small group say, "I'm thankful to be a part of this group because…"
- Intend to be openly encouraging of a ministry, a person, etc.
- Pray for individuals within the church.
- Encourage leaders (small group, fellowship, deacon, elder pastor) at your church by telling them how they're doing a great job. Use specific, concrete examples.
- Send a card or email to pastors/leaders.

Nehemiah

Being Shrewd
Nehemiah 2

Of the many biblical characters that we've looked at thus far, perhaps the one I most identify with is this chapter's hero, Nehemiah. Nehemiah, the Jewish cupbearer to the king of Persia, was the ultimate role model for leadership, ancient or modern. And though we could write on a number of facets in reference to his leadership abilities, the one we want to focus on is his *shrewdness* in dealing with a massive difficulty.

Overcoming Obstacles

Great leaders have always risen to the task of overcoming huge obstacles. Think of the problems that were thrust upon our past American presidents.

General George Washington faced the daunting task of leading a rag tag band against the British Army, the most superior armed force in the world at that time. His military skill and commanding leadership led the Americans to victory, which caused the newly founded republic to call him to become our first president.

Abraham Lincoln presided over a divided nation with the southern half ready to secede from the Union. And though his leadership led to the defeat of the South, Lincoln also oversaw the initial process of reconciliation and the healing of a broken people.

Franklin Delano Roosevelt didn't let his crippling disease stop him from pulling the nation out of economic depression. And it certainly didn't slow him down when he took America into, which resulted in an ultimate victory in, World War II.

Assessing the Problem

Even though he was never a sovereign of a nation, Nehemiah exemplified the same traits of greatness during his troubling situation. Let's go back to his time and review his dilemma in which he demonstrated incredible leadership.

While serving in Persia, he got a message from his brother concerning the sad state of his home city of Jerusalem. Chapter 1 of his book records that Nehemiah wept, mourned, fasted, and prayed over the precarious situation of Jerusalem's walls being in complete ruin, thus leaving the city defenseless against its enemies. What could be done to possibly save his beloved city? And who was he, just one man, living 800 miles away, a VIP in the Persian palace, but a nobody in distant Palestine? What could he possibly do to help out his people and his hometown? The answer, surprisingly, is found in a parable of Jesus:

> *"Jesus told this story to his disciples: 'There was a certain rich man who had a manager handling his affairs. One day*

> a report came that the manager was wasting his employer's money. So the employer called him in and said, "What's this I hear about you? Get your report in order, because you are going to be fired."
>
> 'The manager thought to himself, Now what? My boss has fired me. I don't have the strength to dig ditches, and I'm too proud to beg. Ah, I know how to ensure that I'll have plenty of friends who will give me a home when I am fired.
>
> 'So he invited each person who owed money to his employer to come and discuss the situation. He asked the first one, "How much do you owe him?" The man replied, "I owe him 800 gallons of olive oil." So the manager told him, "Take the bill and quickly change it to 400 gallons."
>
> '"And how much do you owe my employer?" he asked the next man. "I owe him 1,000 bushels of wheat," was the reply. "Here," the manager said, "take the bill and change it to 800 bushels."'[77]

Now comes the time of reckoning. The master found out what the steward did, and look at how he responded...

> "The rich man had to admire the dishonest rascal for being so shrewd. And it is true that the children of this world are more shrewd in dealing with the world around them than are the children of the light."[78]

---

[77] Luke 16:1-7 NLT
[78] Luke 16:8 NLT

This parable introduces us to an unsavory business manager. However, Jesus' focus was not on this man's loose morals, but rather, on his apparent shrewdness. He used his position; he utilized those connections which were available to him to get ahead, and the master, a representation of God, *admires* him for it!

You can almost hear the final words the boss has for his conniving employee: "I've got to hand it to you; you pulled one over on me. What you did behind my back with my two clients...that was smart. You're going to go places. You're going to succeed...just not with me. Now get out of my office!"

A Call for Shrewdness

What Jesus teaches us in this parable is that his followers, if they are to be effective for Kingdom work, must be shrewd. As a Christian for the last thirty years, half of that time as a businessman and the other half as a pastor, I've witnessed how people, both believers and non-believers, deal with adverse situations. And generally, I've found that non-believers are much shrewder in how they deal with sticky challenges than believers. That, in essence, is what the Lord is saying when he declares that the people of this world are more shrewd in dealing with their own kind than people of light. We just don't show ourselves to be as smart as those pagans when it comes to being savvy!

Our Lord commends believers who are shrewd when dealing with those who are of the world. He admires the Christian consumer who fights the auto dealership to take off the extra charge that was not discussed on the contract.

He lauds the Christian job hunter who diligently researches the competition she has for a particular position and contrasts their weaknesses against her strengths in her interview. The Lord applauds the Christian student who is able to cajole his teacher into bumping up his grade on a research project. Jesus summed it up this way: "Be as innocent as a dove in regard to our *faith*, but shrewd as a serpent in dealing with the *people* of this *world*."

> **Jesus wants us to be as innocent as a dove in regard to our *faith*, but shrewd as a serpent in dealing with the *people* of this *world*.**

Why bring up this topic of shrewdness? It's because our hero, Nehemiah, in chapter 2 of his book, is a glowing example of how a child of light is shrewd in dealing with those in the world. Let's begin with the first two verses:

> "In the month of Nisan in the twentieth year of King Artaxerxes, when wine was brought for him, I took the wine and gave it to the king. I had not been sad in his presence before; so the king asked me, 'Why does your face look so sad when you are not ill? This can be nothing but sadness of heart.' I was very much afraid."[79]

Four months have passed since our introduction to the cupbearer of the King of Persia. Nehemiah was concerned about the situation in Jerusalem all this time, and we can presume that behind closed doors in the seclusion of his room, he wept, mourned, fasted, and prayed for the city that he loved. Outwardly however, before the king, his demeanor carried forth as if everything was just fine and

---

[79] Nehemiah 2:1-2 NIV

dandy. Eventually, as the days of frustration turned into weeks, and the weeks into months, this burden in his heart began to percolate from deep within his soul, to be obvious by the furrow of his brow. After testing the wine, the royal cupbearer brought it to his king. We surmise that Artaxerxes may have been a sensitive sovereign because he immediately noticed that his trusted servant was disturbed. Literally in the Hebrew, he says to Nehemiah, your face looks *bad*.

Fear began to overcome Nehemiah. Why? The text doesn't directly tell us, but we can ascertain the possibility of three reasons:

1. Because he was the cupbearer, a negative demeanor might be interpreted as dissatisfaction with his job, which might anger the king.

2. The king was in the middle of a festivity, and a sad face might bring the king down in spirit.

3. Nehemiah had been planning what he wanted to do for four months, and now was the moment of truth – he had to bring his request before the king.

It is at this point that we begin to witness the shrewdness of Nehemiah in regard to dealing with people.

Four Ways of Being Shrewd to Accomplish God's Work

1. **A shrewd person chooses words** *carefully.*

> "...but I said to the king, 'May the king live forever! Why should my face not look sad when the city where my fathers are buried lies in ruins, and its gates have been destroyed by fire?'
>
> The king said to me, 'What is it you want?' Then I prayed to the God of heaven, and I answered the king, 'If it pleases the king and if your servant has found favor in his sight, let him send me to the city in Judah where my fathers are buried so that I can rebuild it.'
>
> Then the king, with the queen sitting beside him, asked me, 'How long will your journey take, and when will you get back?' It pleased the king to send me; so I set a time."[80]

Note how Nehemiah approached the subject of Jerusalem. First of all, he *praised* the king. *"May the king live forever!"* Sure, it may seem like a simple case of the servant sucking up to the sovereign, but it certainly set a more positive tone for what Nehemiah wanted to introduce. That's being smart!

Secondly, he never used the word *"Jerusalem,"* but instead refers to it as the city where his fathers were buried, a city located in the region of Judah. What's the big deal in that, you might be asking? The answer is historical.

Ezra 4:8-23 recalls an incident twenty years earlier, where a younger King Artaxerxes received a letter from the ene-

---
[80] Nehemiah 2:3-6 NIV

mies of the Jews stating that the returning Israelites were rebuilding the city of Jerusalem. These troublemakers told the king to research the record books and learn that Jerusalem has always caused the kings and nations of the past a lot of trouble. They urged the king to order them to stop building. The king made that decree, and the text ends by stating that these enemies stopped the Jews from working by force of arms. After twenty years, the walls of the city were still down.

What we're saying is that Nehemiah knew of Artaxerxes' previous decree, and so in asking him to essentially reverse that decree, he's being shrewd in how he approached that sensitive subject, namely by not using the word *"Jerusalem."*

King Artaxerxes was an intelligent man. You don't become and stay king without being smart. He knew where Nehemiah was from. He knew of what city in Judah Nehemiah was speaking, but his affection and respect for Nehemiah, coupled with the cupbearer's fervent prayers to God, caused the king to allow his servant to return to the city of his fathers. His response, *"How long will your journey take and when will you be back?"* is like a teenager who begs his parents over and over to let him go to the Homecoming dance. After an initial response of "No," he gets a subsequent questioning of when is the event and when will he be home? That youth knows that eventually his parents are going to say, "Yes." It's just a matter of time!

> **Sometimes, it's not *what* we have to say, but *how* we say it that makes the difference.**

That's a good lesson for each one of us to learn. We need to go about asking others for favors by choosing our words carefully. Sometimes, it's not *what* we have to say, but *how* we say it that makes the difference. A shrewd person chooses his/her words carefully.

2. A shrewd person covers all of the *bases*.

> *"I also said to him, 'If it pleases the king, may I have letters to the governors of Trans-Euphrates, so that they will provide me safe-conduct until I arrive in Judah?*
>
> *'And may I have a letter to Asaph, keeper of the king's forest, so he will give me timber to make beams for the gates of the citadel by the temple and for the city wall and for the residence I will occupy?' And because the gracious hand of my God was upon me, the king granted my requests."*[81]

After finding favor with the king, Nehemiah took it a step further. Since the king officially decreed that Jerusalem would not be rebuilt, it would also have to be by his authority that Nehemiah would be guaranteed safe passage down to the city.

Throughout the history of their existence as a people, and at that time, Jews had many enemies, and their enemies did not want the Israelites to rebuild Jerusalem. We read later in verses 9 and 10 to find that two men, Sanballat and Tobiah, were harassing Nehemiah. But because the cupbearer carried an official letter from the king, they were not allowed to touch him.

Nehemiah also asked Artaxerxes for a letter addressed to Asaph, the king's "general contractor," to supply lumber for

---

[81] Nehemiah 2:7-8 NIV

rebuilding the walls and gates. Again, Nehemiah knew that his people didn't have the funds or material to do the work, but in thinking ahead, he ensured that, despite his people's poverty, the massive civil works project could commence immediately. That was shrewd.

A shrewd person covers all of the bases. He/she is intelligent enough and thinking ahead to see from where all the potential pitfalls will come. That's what we saw in the parable Jesus gave (located at the introduction of this chapter). The manager called in all of his master's accounts, knowing that these men would someday thank him by offering him either a job or some lucrative deals. He covered his bases.

> **You have to be intelligent enough and think ahead to see from where all the potential pitfalls will come.**

If we lived in a sin-free, perfect world where everyone responded appropriately and with propriety, we wouldn't need to think about all the ways that circumstances can go wrong. People would act with integrity and make things right. But that's not the real world, is it? In business, to ensure that a deal succeeds, you need to be on top of all facets of the transaction – suppliers, shippers, financing, middlemen, owners.

When I worked for a national soft-goods retailer as an Assistant Buyer, the most troublesome transactions were imported clothing traveling across the ocean from the Far East due to arrive right before Christmas. For a retailer that did 25% of annual sales just in those four weeks between Thanksgiving and Christmas Eve, it was imperative that everything went right. If the clothing came in even a few days late, essentially we would be importing automatic Christmas clearance.

That's why I worked with the manufacturer's representative, the shippers, U.S. customs, and even our own distribution centers...everyone...to ensure that our goods made it onto the store floors in a timely manner! And people wonder why the holiday season gets them so stressed out! I gained a few more white hairs during those days.

At those rare times in our lives where everything just goes smoothly without a hitch, don't believe it is dumb luck. A shrewd person covers all the bases.

3. A shrewd person is *discreet*.

> *"I went to Jerusalem, and after staying there three days I set out during the night with a few men. I had not told anyone what my God had put in my heart to do for Jerusalem. There were no mounts with me except the one I was riding on.*
>
> *By night I went out through the Valley Gate toward the Jackal Well and the Dung Gate, examining the walls of Jerusalem, which had been broken down, and its gates, which had been destroyed by fire. Then I moved on toward the Fountain Gate and the King's Pool, but there was not enough room for my mount to get through; so I went up the valley by night, examining the wall. Finally, I turned back and reentered through the Valley Gate.*
>
> *The officials did not know where I had gone or what I was doing, because as yet I had said nothing to the Jews or the*

priests or nobles or officials or any others who would be doing the work."[82]

Nehemiah knew that it would be the Jews in the city who would rebuild the walls with the timber from Asaph, under the protection of King Artaxerxes' decree. But he also recognized that, before any work could commence, he needed to do some research. He arrived in Jerusalem and stayed three days. His intention was two-fold: to gather further information and to engage in intense prayer. Now that he was mentally and spiritually prepared, Nehemiah set out on the third night, taking a few trusted men and only one donkey (horses would have made too much noise), and proceeded with a thorough inspection of the walls and gates.

Why did he go at night? For three reasons: 1) He didn't want to alarm his enemies by inspecting the walls during the day; 2) He didn't want to cause curiosity among the Jews who didn't know why he was necessarily there; 3) Most importantly, before he could approach his people about doing the work, he wanted to know exactly what needed to be done.

Nothing is worse than having a boss demand for you to complete an assignment, but he doesn't have a clue about what it takes to get the job done.

In all these different ways, Nehemiah demonstrated himself to be discreet.

---

[82] Nehemiah 2:11-16 NIV

4. A shrewd person knows how to *inspire*.

> *"Then I said to them, 'You see the trouble we are in: Jerusalem lies in ruins, and its gates have been burned with fire. Come, let us rebuild the wall of Jerusalem, and we will no longer be in disgrace.'*
>
> *I also told them about the gracious hand of my God upon me and what the king had said to me. They replied, 'Let us start rebuilding.' So they began this good work.*
>
> *But when Sanballat the Horonite, Tobiah the Ammonite official and Geshem the Arab heard about it, they mocked and ridiculed us. 'What is this you are doing?' they asked. 'Are you rebelling against the king?'*
>
> *I answered them by saying, 'The God of heaven will give us success. We his servants will start rebuilding, but as for you, you have no share in Jerusalem or any claim or historic right to it.'"*[83]

After making the secret inspection, Nehemiah was now prepared to share his plan openly with his people. Again, note his shrewdness in how he went about inspiring his people to rally to the cause. First, he appealed to their sense of *self-determination*.

We need to remind ourselves that those who dwelled in Jerusalem all those years had become numb to the sorry state of their city. It's the proverbial frog in the kettle scenario. The frog will immediately jump out of a pot of hot water. But place him in cold water and raise the temperature very slowly, and he'll eventually boil to death. The

---

[83] Nehemiah 2:17-20 NIV

Israelites, after years of status quo defenselessness, were unaware of their pathetic situation.

Unaware of Our Sad Situation

By way of application, many times we become callous to issues within the church. Maybe you're like me, in that you've been a part of your church so long that the facilities seem like a second home. The sanctuary is as familiar and comfortable as your own family room. But like our own home, things in the church can break down, become neglected, and because we've lived with it for so long, we have become unaware of the problem.

When you take a closer look, you realize that the pews are filthy. The door to the last stall in the main bathroom sticks. The latch is missing on one of the cribs in the nursery. These items have been in disrepair for so long, church members and even the staff members don't notice them any more…but newcomers do! And I thank God for those bold new visitors who are willing to mention these issues to the usher who just welcomed them into the sanctuary, or to the preaching pastor, whose hand they just shook on the way out, or even to put a comment on a visitor card.

When I go away on vacation, I love to visit other churches. I always am blessed by seeing how others run their ministry, and it's great to hear another voice other than my own declaring God's truth. One time, I visited a church and I noticed many people talking amongst themselves, but no one greeted me. In the service, they had all the visitors stand to acknowledge us, and a few came and shook my hand, but then they went back to business as usual.

Finally, the presider invited all the newcomers to come to a room where they could get to know others in the church. After the service I went to that room, but no one greeted me. A few weeks later, the Senior Pastor called me and thanked me for coming. I told him I appreciated his preaching, and I could have left it at that. But I decided to tell him about how I was welcomed in the church. He acknowledged that they had problems being hospitable to newcomers, as the church was a more "family–oriented" ministry, and people were used to those who'd grown up in the congregation.

> **Leaders need to be able to hear the not-so-pretty realities of their ministries.**

I can tell you as a pastor, that I appreciate people who are willing to tell us the truth in love. Leaders need to be able to hear the not-so-pretty realities of their ministries.

Thank God for honest people! They play the role of Nehemiah when he says to the Israelites, "We are a disgrace to our enemies because our city is defenseless. Let *us* rebuild the walls and gates."

Did you note the use of the word *"us"* instead of *"you"*? As an effective leader, Nehemiah always addressed himself with his people collectively. It wasn't "I" or "you," rather it was "we." We're in this together!

As a young pastor, I remember coming to this very realization and changing how I addressed my congregation in my sermons. It went from what were *you* going to do with God's truth, to what are *we* going to do with God's truth?!!! Who do *we* turn to when *we* struggle with sin? How will *we* resolve this conflict within the church? Let *us* celebrate God's grace together! Inclusiveness spurs on camaraderie and a sense of belonging. Nehemiah was shrewd in this way.

Including God

A second means through which Nehemiah inspired his people is that he invoked the *name* of God. It wasn't about the cupbearer being the Savior for his people, but rather, about Yahweh providing the way. Nehemiah spoke in verse 18 of God's gracious hand being with him. This certainly encouraged the Israelites because they knew that what they were about to embark upon would be approved and sanctioned by God.

No Negative Nellies!

The final way that Nehemiah inspired his people is that he minimized *negativity*. Our old friends, Sanballat and Tobiah, as well as a new antagonist, Geshem, were endeavoring to discourage the troops. These enemies of God's people wanted the Jews to second guess their desire to rebuild the walls. They wanted them to think of it not as urban renewal, but rather, as a provocation against the king. Nehemiah cut them off by invoking God's name, inspiring them to success. *"We will start rebuilding"*...he helps them to envision the possibility, and these enemies of his people will have no claim to, nor will they be allowed to impede, what is accomplished.

Nehemiah was truly an inspirational leader. Throughout this whole chapter, we have seen him use his intellectual capabilities, his past experiences, his accumulated wisdom, his role and position, his motivational skills, and especially his trust in God, to bring about his goal of rebuilding the walls of Jerusalem. That's being shrewd. That's being smart for God.

Personal Testimony

I am reminded of the history of my home church back in Northern California. Our Senior Pastor desired to move the church from an urban setting to a less-populated suburban unincorporated town. He shared that back in the 1960s, they were looking at the hills and they wanted to build a large church atop one of them. The problem was that the several dozen acres of land were owned by four separate farmers. Our pastor had a vision from the Lord to build on this prime location because everyone who passed by on the intersection of two major freeways would see the church and be reminded of God.

God was with him for the pastor was able to persuade the four non-believing farmers, independent of each other, to sell the land. And what makes this more remarkable is that there would be no church unless all of them sold their respective properties. After the unlikely purchase of the land, to make the site viable, a million yards of dirt needed to be removed. The cost was a dollar per yard, quite a bit of money back in the '60s.

God had that arranged. A new football/baseball stadium was being built nearby and they needed, you guessed it, a million yards of dirt. Through shrewd negotiation, the church "graciously" gave their dirt for the stadium site, which of course, saved them a million dollars.

A lot of people were involved in the building of my home church, but the credit, through God's benevolence, ultimately goes to my senior pastor. He was a man of vision. He was shrewd for God.

Being smart in matters isn't just important at high levels. God may be calling you to be shrewd for his Kingdom. As a student, he may be calling you to implement a Christian program on campus. Maybe he wants you to create a bridge between your church and a secular organization. Maybe he wants you to coordinate fundraising for a special missions project. Whatever it is, he's calling you to be shrewd, to use your position, your possession, your personality, to do something great for him.

Taking Time to Get Real

Heart-to-Heart

You might be thinking that this chapter is the least applicable to you. I'm not a leader. I have no influence over others. It sounds very humble, but it's simply not true. If you're a husband, you're called to lead in your home. If you're a parent, you lead your family. Teaching children's Sunday school is significant. You are shaping the minds of the next generation. You may head up a project at your children's school, or at the church, or you lead a small group. You are a leader. The question is how effective are you in your leadership?

Take some time to meditate and think about the various roles of leadership you play in your life. Ask the Lord to reveal areas of victory, as well as areas of challenge. Ask him to show you how to be more effective.

Questions for Discussion

- Do you choose your words carefully? Are you judicious in what you say, or do you suffer from foot-in-mouth disease? Give examples either way of how you communicate to others.

- When dealing with potential problems and difficult people, are you more apt to react in a *fly-by-the-seat-of-your-pants* method, or are you more likely to be methodical? How has either approach served you well? How has it made dealing with issues more difficult?

- Would you consider yourself to be a discreet person? By discreet, we're speaking of being judicious in what we say and to whom we say it. Give examples of your discretion or lack of discretion and how it affected your relationship(s).

- Would you consider your church to have a strong sense of community? How would an outsider be treated in the first few months of attending your church? Even if your church is doing a good job, what further steps could be taken to make your church even friendlier?

- What is the most inspiring aspect of the way Nehemiah went about getting the walls rebuilt in Jerusalem? How can that aspect be applied in your own life?

Memory Verse: Ephesians 4:29

Do not let any unwholesome talk come out of your mouths, but only what is helpful for building others up according to their needs, that it may benefit those who listen.

Heartwork

Maybe this chapter has made you think of areas within your church that are in disrepair. Get together with a like-minded group of people (perhaps your small group or Sunday School class) and make a list of things in the church that need to be fixed. Work with the church leadership, if necessary, but if you and your friends can take care of it on your own, it would be a real blessing to the congregation and an inspiration that they, too, can accomplish great things for God.

Daniel

Either/Or versus Both/And
Daniel 1

You've just picked up this book and have decided to read this final chapter. You're doing this because God is gracious and has given you the free will to make choices. Instead of reading this book, you could have grabbed the TV remote, channel-surfed, and chosen from a myriad of programs to watch. You could have gone into the kitchen, opened the fridge, and created your own unique sandwich. You could have taken a walk around the neighborhood, crammed for an upcoming math test, or got online and blogged. It is your choice.

Decisions, Decisions, Decisions

Life is full of them. Consciously, or more likely unconsciously, you've made dozens of decisions this very day – how many times you'd hit the snooze alarm, or what clothes you chose to wear, what to eat for breakfast, or whether to fill up the gas tank today or tomorrow when the gauge tells you that you're driving on fumes.

Maybe you're like me, you're the type of person who makes decisions quickly and doesn't regret a choice that is less than perfect. I'm a tried-and-true type of guy. I can go to the same restaurant three days in a row (my choice), order the same number ten dish (again, my choice), and be very content. But that's me and for the handful of you who are like me. For the vast majority of humanity, trying to decide might be a little more difficult. It's difficult because you realize that for you to make a specific choice means that you have to give up other options – and you want to keep all those options open.

For example, take the high school senior who has to make a decision on what to do with his life. 1) Does he pursue entrance into a university? And if he decides to further his education, which college does he attend? If he decides to attend a university and it's a local school, he'll have to decide whether to live at home and save money (not to mention having a gracious mother who prepares home cooked meals) or have more freedom living in a dorm (but lose out on someone else doing his laundry). Each option has its pros and cons, and he has to weigh all of them and decide. Decisions – in most cases they are part of an either/or situation. Either you choose one or the other; and try as you may, the reality is that you just can't have them both.

> **Decisions need to be made between the *sacred* and the *secular*, between the things of *God* and the things of *men*.**

And while life is full of give-and-takes in regard to decision making, the ones we want to talk about in this final chapter are the decisions that need to be made between the *sacred* and the *secular*, between the things of *God* and the things of *men*.

Perhaps you've heard of the phrase *"spiritual disciplines."* By spiritual disciplines, we are speaking of the habits and intentional purposes by people of faith to nurture a closer relationship with God. Some of those disciplines may be familiar to you: prayer, Scripture reading, fasting, meditation, and seclusion.

Now in regard to decision making, let's choose Scripture reading as an example. We know that a good habit is to have a daily devotion, a set time each day where we allow God to speak to us through the reading of the Bible and for us to communicate with him through prayer. Most of us have the best of intentions to maintain this spiritual discipline, but if you're like me, you find constant outside pressures preventing you from maintaining any kind of devotional consistency.

It's an either/or situation. Either you spend time reading your Bible or you read your English assignment. Either you spend time talking to God or you spend time talking with your friends. Either you spend time serving in the church or you spend time putting a few more hours on the job. We see decisions between God and man as either/or, and many times, if we're honest, God ends up on the losing side.

> **We see decisions between God and man as either/or, and many times, if we're honest, God ends up on the losing side.**

What we're going to observe in the first chapter of the book of Daniel is that it doesn't have to be an either/or situation; with God, it can be both/and. You can have both your devotion and ace your mid-term. You can serve in the church and complete your work project. You can have your cake and eat it, too. You don't believe it? Then let's move on and see how this works.

The Removal

> "The Lord gave Jehoiakim into Nebuchadnezzar's hand..."[84]

The year was 605 B.C. and the nation of Judah had ignored the warnings of the prophets, Jeremiah and Habakkuk, in worshiping idols. The people weren't necessarily all at fault, for they were simply carrying out the actions of their king, Jehoiakim, who decided to reject Yahweh and follow the pagan gods of the surrounding nations. Jehoiakim gave up the religious reforms of his godly father, Josiah, and instead followed Egyptian cult practices. He went further down the path of evil by shedding innocent blood and had the prophet Uriah murdered for opposing him. In addition, further thumbing his nose at God, Jehoiakim attacked Jeremiah the prophet and personally burnt the scroll that was read to him. As to how he treated his own people, being a self-absorbed man, he imposed heavy taxes in order to build costly palaces for himself.

Because of all this, the Lord brought judgment upon the king and his people for their unfaithfulness.

> "And the Lord gave Jehoiakim, king of Judah into Nebuchadnezzar's hand..."

---

[84] Daniel 1:1 NIV

From a human perspective, it would seem as if Judah fell because of Nebuchadnezzar's military prowess. But the text makes it clear that it was the Lord, not Nebuchadnezzar, who subdued Jehoiakim. Have you ever had a person pop on over to your house uninvited? In the same way, like an unwelcome guest, Nebuchadnezzar came into Palestine, made a mess of everything, and left without saying, "Thank you." You read on further in the text that he took two precious things from the Hebrews:

1. **The religious articles.**

> "And the Lord delivered Jehoiakim king of Judah into his hand, along with some of the articles from the temple of God. These he carried off to the temple of his god in Babylonia and put in the treasure house of his god."[85]

These items were taken not only for their monetary value, but just as importantly, as a form of humiliation in that Nebuchadnezzar desired to disrespect the God of the Jews.

2. **Their *most promising young men*.**

> "Then the king ordered Ashpenaz, chief of his court officials, to bring in some of the Israelites from the royal family and the nobility – young men without any physical defect, handsome, showing aptitude for every kind of learning,

---
[85] Daniel 1:2 NIV

well informed, quick to understand, and qualified to serve in the king's palace."[86]

Scholars will advocate that a nation's true strength lies not within its natural resources or vastness of territory, but rather, within its people. Nebuchadnezzar evidently believed this to be true, and that's why he had these Jewish superstars carted back to Babylon. These young men were the cream of the Hebrew crop:

- They were of *nobility* – These young men had a name for themselves among the Jews. The ancient paparazzi would have dogged them incessantly, trying to capture their faces and exploits in their national tabloids.

- They were *handsome* – When these young men walked about town, the hearts of the young maidens would flutter. They were eye candy to the unattached ladies.

- They were *intelligent* – They all had IQs over 150 and high scores on their SATs that would gain them admission to any ancient Ivy League school. They were the class valedictorians. They won first prize at the science fair. And not only were they book smart, but they also knew how to use their wealth of knowledge; they had the wisdom to discern right from wrong. They were young men of good character.

---

[86] Daniel 1:3-4 NIV

These men were the elite of the elite. They were the best the country had to offer. For you fathers, you aspire for your son to become like these men. For you mothers, these are the type of men you'd want your daughters to marry.

Nebuchadnezzar took quite a few of these young men with him, but note that only four are mentioned in our text. Their names were Daniel, Hananiah, Mishael, and Azariah. And the reason why their names are recorded in our Scripture, and not any of the others, is because not only were they of nobility, handsome, and intelligent, but they were also, most importantly, *godly*.

> **Their names are recorded in Scripture because not only were they of *nobility, handsome,* and *intelligent*; but most important, they were *godly*.**

A little Hebrew lesson gives us an indication of their character. Each of their names speaks of their spiritual connection with the Lord:

Daniel – *God has judged.*
Hananiah – *Yahweh has been gracious.*
Mishael – *Who is what God is?*
Azariah – *Yahweh has helped.*

Their names convey to us that their parents desired to nurture their faith in Yahweh. Perhaps it's the same thing for you, if you grew up in a devout Christian home where your parents gave you a biblical name. In my home church, we have children named Isaiah, Enoch, David, Benjamin,

Rebekah. I spoke at a church retreat where one of the girls was even named Dorcas![87]

Do you know what your name means? Many times, parents will choose a name for their child not just because it sounds good, but because they would desire that their offspring might take on the characteristics of that name. We named our first daughter Bethany, which means "house of figs." There's really no spiritual meaning there, but we tell others that we named her Bethany because Bethany was the city that was the home of Jesus' friends, Martha, Mary and Lazarus. And likewise, we want to remind Bethany that she, too, is a friend of Jesus. Bethany was given a Chinese middle name as well, En-Ci, which was chosen by her maternal grandparents. It is translated as "kindness," and was selected because it is one of the fruit of the Spirit.[88]

In any case, these four young men were given new names by the Babylonians, heathen names that were meant to take away some of the spiritual emphasis on their faith in Yahweh. They were renamed Belteshazzar, Shadrach, Meshach, and Abednego.

These four teenagers, along with their friends, were given a three year crash course in Babylonian culture. The curriculum included subjects on agriculture, architecture, astrology, astronomy, law, mathematics, as well learning the difficult language of Akkadian. They were given personal tutors to assist them, rich food to nourish them, and wine from the king's own personal cellar to satisfy their thirst. Nothing was withheld from these promising young diplomats.

---

[87] See Acts 9:36, 39
[88] Galatians 5:22-23 NIV

And what was the prize? To win a spot in the king's court. To be part of the elite. To have positions of power, prestige, and authority. To live in affluence and to have the admiration of all the people. In other words, this would be a parent's dream for his/her child.

It sounds too good to be true. You're carted off from your family and homeland to become part of the elite of the empire. But there's a catch and herein lies the potential tension for these four young men. They have come from a godly background, nurtured by their parents from a very young age to remain devout and righteous to the God of the Jews. Now they have the opportunity to make it big in the world. Sure, they were the top students in their respective high schools; that was a piece of cake. But now they're being pitted against the best of the best. Any of these teens would have been readily accepted at Harvard, Yale, or Stanford.

The pressure to do well was confronted by the conviction to remain true to their God. They were to be given the finest education, allowed to live in an environment which was enjoyable and free of care, and given the opportunity to compete for some of the highest positions in the land. Could these young men hold onto their faith, and yet still do well in their educations and careers? Would they choose to go God's way and perhaps miss out on these high job opportunities, or would they choose to forego their faith and devote themselves entirely to occupational aspirations?

How about you? What is your priority in life? Do you view your life as an either/or situation? Yes, I'd like to keep a consistent devotional prayer life, but I need to devote more time to study. Yes, I'd like to serve more diligently in the church, but I need to put more time at the office. Yes, I'd like to give more liberally to God's work abroad, but I have bills to pay, a mortgage to pay off, and kids to feed.

The reality of life seems to be made up of choosing between the secular and the sacred, between the world and worship, between the things of God and the things of men. And many times, if we're brutally honest, more often than not, we choose *Babylon* over the *Kingdom of God*. We desire the goodies over devotion to God. And that's the decision these four young men had to face. Let's see what they chose to do.

> **Many times, if we're brutally honest, we choose *Babylon* over the *Kingdom of God*.**

The Resolution

"God granted Daniel favor and compassion..."[89]

Daniel 8:8 begins with, *"But Daniel made up his mind..."* Literally, the text could read, "Daniel *set upon his heart* that he would not defile himself with the king's choice food or with the wine which he was offered."

Maybe you were blessed by being taught Bible stories in children's Sunday School. You might have read this passage many times and think that King Nebuchadnezzar had chosen only four from Judah to be in his courts. But that's not true. David and his three friends were four of many who were taken from Judah (you'll recall verse 6, *"Now among them..."*). The reason these four were mentioned is

---

[89] Daniel 1:9 NIV

because they chose to do things differently than their other Jewish friends.

Daniel resolved, made up his mind, set upon his heart, not to defile himself with Babylonian food and drink, not to taint himself with that which was apart from God. He sought to keep himself faithful to the God of his forefathers. The food offered to him was most likely sacrificed to the Babylonian idols, Marduk, Nebo, and Ishtar. The wine was used as libations for these gods. Daniel obeyed the Deuteronomic and Levitical laws, which said to abstain from eating and drinking unclean food.

So how did Daniel try to get out of eating this food and drinking the wine? *"...and he* [Daniel] *asked the chief official for permission not to defile himself this way."*[90]

And how did this chief official respond to their request? Was he gracious and understanding? Did he agree to their appeal? No, it was God who is gracious and understanding. *"Now God had caused the official to show favor and sympathy to Daniel..."*[91]

We can't really hold it against Ashpenaz, the chief official. He reported to a higher authority and realized that, if these young men looked tired and weak, it would cost him not only his job, but more importantly his head! Daniel was empathetic. He asked this officer to test them – with just ten days of vegetable and water – and compare their appearance with the others. The implication, as well as the test for their faith, was that if they didn't look better, Ashpenaz was free do as he pleased. The commander agreed to the test because of God. And the results were that, even after only ten days

---

[90] Daniel 1:8b NIV
[91] Daniel 1:9 NIV

of a non-Atkins diet, they looked fatter and healthier than the others:

> "So the guard took away their choice food and the wine they were to drink and gave them vegetables instead."[92]

They say that hindsight is always 20/20. Let's go back to verse 8 and remind ourselves of Daniel's commitment to spiritual purity: *"But Daniel made up his mind, set upon his heart, resolved, not to defile himself by eating the food and drinking the wine."* We've mentioned earlier that all of us have free will, and that was the same for this pagan official, as well. What if Ashpenaz had not agreed to let Daniel and his friends have the vegetables and water? What would these young men have done? What would you have done?

Daniel and his friends were not willing to compromise their faith. They probably would have been executed immediately for their disobedience to the king's command. Now if we were to place ourselves in their situation, we would have said something like this: "Either you let us abstain from your food and wine or we'll continue to eat your food and drink your wine...*but we won't like it!*" That would put this chief official and King Nebuchadnezzar in their places! If we were honest with ourselves, very few of us would be willing to die in order to stay obedient to God's commands.

---

[92] Daniel 1:16 NIV

Lessons Learned from Daniel and His Friends

1. God desires to bless my faithfulness.

We see in this narrative that the Lord moved the heart of the official such that these young men didn't have to take such dire steps. It's the same for us today. We will be blessed if we remain faithful to the Lord's commands. That doesn't mean, however, that we won't suffer harm. God can certainly protect our lives – we see that with Daniel and his friends. But he can also allow a godly life to be taken. There have been thousands of Christian martyrs throughout the last two millennia who could give testimony of God's faithfulness to their obedience.

The bottom line is that whether God protects us or allows us to suffer for obedience, most of us have never gotten to the point of even putting ourselves to the test. We take the path of either/or and never get challenged with both/and. We don't allow the testing, and thus have not experienced the reward of maintaining faithfulness to the Lord.

2. A positive testimony can offset potential testing.

These four young men left a positive impression on Nebuchadnezzar's chief official. Most likely, he saw a difference between men of conviction and men who sought compromise. Maybe he couldn't put his finger on the difference – he might not have ever noticed them praying regularly or reciting the Torah. But by their actions, by the way they lived their lives, he was willing to honor their request and essentially put his life in their hands. We call this sometimes intangible quality *trust*. Although the officer didn't agree with their beliefs, their integrity and demeanor led him to trust them completely.

Can you say the same for yourself in terms of the nonbelievers in whom you have contact: among your relatives, at school, at your job, or in your neighborhood? Do you see them acting differently toward you than to your peers because of the positive testimony you have as a Christ-follower? Are you known for being virtuous, a person of character?

The Result

> "*God gave them knowledge and understanding in every branch of literature and wisdom…*"[93]

> "*And Daniel could understand visions and dreams of all kinds. At the end of the time set by the king to bring them in, the chief official presented them to Nebuchadnezzar. The king talked with them, and he found none equal to Daniel, Hananiah, Mishael and Azariah; so they entered the king's service. In every matter of wisdom and understanding about which the king questioned them, he found them ten times better than all the magicians and enchanters in his whole kingdom. And Daniel remained there until the first year of King Cyrus.*"[94]

---

[93] Daniel 1:17 NIV
[94] Daniel 1:17-21 NIV

God gave them knowledge and understanding in *every* branch of literature and wisdom.

A question for reminder: Who gave these four young men their intelligence and wisdom? Was it the Babylonian school district, the good tutors? Was it the king's chief official? No! It was God! The Lord alone is the giver of all good things! But somehow, we think that the blessings of life come from ourselves because of our own efforts or perhaps the efforts of our involved parents, a motivating teacher, a hard-driving coach, a mentoring boss. That's why we live a life of either/or:

> "I can't make Bible study, I've got school homework." Either you cram for hours or resolve to learn more about God.
>
> "I can't make my mid-week cell group meeting because I want to meet with my non-church friends." Either you party like a pagan or you fellowship with other believers.
>
> "I want to keep consistency with reading my Bible every day, but I'm not getting to bed early enough." Either you spend more time sleeping or studying your Bible.

Either/or, either/or, either/or.

Here's the message that God has for each of us this very day: Not either/or, but both/and! God was, is, and will always be in control of our lives. The Lord was in control of Daniel and his friends' lives:

"The Lord gave Jehoiakim..."

"God granted Daniel favor..."

"God gave them intelligence..."

Here is what the almighty, sovereign Lord is telling each of us today: "If you will choose to worship me, honor me, put me first in your life, then I will bless you with the desires of your heart. If you choose to pursue the things of the world, you lose me. But if you choose to pursue me, you get me, and the desires of your heart." For anyone with an ounce of common sense, it seems like a no-brainer decision.

This same truth that is declared in the Old Testament reverberates throughout Scripture and is echoed from the lips of Jesus himself, when he asked, "Why are you anxious about your life, what you will wear, what you will eat, (or for that matter what grades you get, what school you go to, what job he'll give you, or who will be your mate)? I take care of the birds; I arrange the lilies of the field...everything is in the palm of my hand. So don't be anxious then, saying, 'What shall we eat?' or 'What shall we drink?' or 'With what shall we clothe ourselves?' For all these things the non-believers eagerly seek; for your heavenly father knows that you need all these things. But seek first His kingdom and His righteousness; and all these things shall be given to you."[95]

---

[95] Paraphrased from Matthew 6:25ff

Bringing It All Together

When I think of a man who sought God first in all aspects of his life, I'm reminded of Eric Liddell. Nicknamed the Flying Scotsman, he was nobly portrayed in the movie *Chariots of Fire*. This was a man who pursued God first and Olympic glory second. In 1924, he was expected to handily win the 100-meter sprint. But there was a problem – one of the trials was scheduled for Sunday, and he was under the conviction that God did not want him to race on the Sabbath. So he declined the opportunity.

People throughout the world at that time were debating whether the day of the race should be changed, but the Olympic committee, and rightly so, refused to alter the schedule. Everything Liddell had worked for would be in vain – the years of training, the expense, the time…all would be a waste. Why? Because of his conviction.

> **Eric Liddell was going after Jesus first, the Olympic gold second, and not the other way around.**

Eric Liddell was going after Jesus first, the Olympic gold second, and not the other way around. He chose to not pursue the path of either/or. But would God bless him with a both/and?

In the end, Liddell did get to compete in the Olympics, however, not in the 100-meter sprint. Instead, he competed in the 400-meter run, which for anyone who understands track, it is a race that requires much more stamina. In the finals, during the last turn, he showed the world, once again, his uncanny running style. Toward the end of the race, his head jerked back and his arms flew open, a style that so characterized his relationship with God. Quoted one man,

"He ran with faith. He didn't even look where he was going."

Eric Liddell set a new world record in the 400-meters and won Olympic gold. Liddell pursued a path of both/and. He understood better than any other person the words of his Lord:

> *"Seek first the kingdom of God, and his righteousness, and all these other things will be added unto you."*[96]

---

[96] Matthew 6:33 NIV

Taking Time to Get Real

Heart-to-Heart

Put down the book and sit back. Close your eyes and ask the Holy Spirit to illuminate some truths from the story of Daniel and his friends. Begin a dialogue with the Lord. Ask him to reveal to you areas where you've compromised your faith, where you lived a life of either/or.

Questions for Discussion

- Go back to the text of Daniel 1 and reread the passage. Especially key in on the verses that emphasize God's control (verses 2, 9, 17). Ponder the times or incidences in your life and discern when it was God, not yourself, who brought about blessing and safety.

- When you think of the success you've had in your education, athletic endeavors, work or family life, who have you given credit to in the past? Can you see from Daniel 1 how God has influenced, used, or altered situations, or people to bring about what has happened in your life? How so?

- Ponder the saying, "Do your best and give God the rest." Would you say that you have essentially lived up this motto? If so, how? What does Daniel 1 teach you about the truth of this saying? Develop a better motto that fits in well with the truths found in Daniel 1.

- Think of the bank teller that you see regularly, or your child's teacher, or your aerobics instructor, or your co-worker, or fellow student. How would they describe the person you are? Do you think they would trust you with their possessions or secrets? Why or why not?

- Put yourself in the place of Daniel at the beginning of the chapter. What would you have worried about? What do you worry about right now? What does Daniel 1 tell you about your worrying?

Memory Verse: *Matthew 6:31-34*

So do not worry, saying, "What shall we eat?" or "What shall we drink?" or "What shall we wear?" For the pagans run after all these things, and your heavenly Father knows that you need them. But seek first his kingdom and his righteousness, and all these things will be given to you as well. Therefore do not worry about tomorrow, for tomorrow will worry about itself. Each day has enough trouble of its own.

Heartwork

Take out a sheet of paper and draw a line down the middle. On the left side, title the column, "Areas where I struggle in my spiritual life." Begin to write down areas of struggle for you. On the right side, title it, "Things that cause me to struggle spiritually." Using the items you wrote down in the first column, write down specific things, people, attitudes, thoughts, actions that cause you to struggle in those areas, that rob you of spiritual vitality. Pray over the sheet and ask God to help you reprioritize your life.

Conclusion

We come to the conclusion of this book, but not the conclusion of the story of these ten who have come before us. Your life, how you live it, will be a continuation of their legacy, a legacy which will be passed on to future generations, should Jesus decide to hold off his return. Hopefully, as you go forward, you will live a life where you demonstrate more faith and less flaws.

But during those times when you feel like you're backpedaling in your faith, remember that the Christian life is a process of growth. You are a work in progress and God isn't done with you yet. Keep on keeping on. Reread some of the stories of those individuals who floundered for a while, but in the end, came away victorious.

Like Eric Liddell, you are in a race, a race that ends with your last breath. This is a race that offers no medals or accolades from the crowds. It is a race where the only acknowledgement of victory comes from a lone voice. Let us all strive to hear the words from our Lord and Master, *"Well done, good and faithful servant!"*

Don't look back. Keep your eye on the prize...

"Forgetting what is behind and straining toward what is ahead, I press on toward the goal to win the prize for which God has called me heavenward in Christ Jesus."[97]

May God bless you,
Derek Quan

---

[97] Philippians 3:13-14 NIV

Intermedia Publishing Group
Publishing That Works For You

Would you like Derek Quan to speak to your group or event? If so, contact Larry Davis at (623) 337-8710 or email ldavis@intermediapr.com.

If you want to purchase bulk copies of *The Faithful and the Flawed* or buy another book for a friend, get it now at www.imprbooks.com.

If you have a book you would like to publish, contact **Larry Davis, Intermedia Publishing Group** at (623) 337-8710 or email ldavis@intermediapr.com.